Éléonore Muhidine (ed.)
Indian Architecture in Postcards

Éléonore Muhidine (PhD), born in 1988, is a research assistant at the Department City Building Culture at Fachhochschule Potsdam. She studied art history in Paris, Rennes and Berlin. Her research focuses on 20th century architecture and urban planning in Germany and India.

Éléonore Muhidine (ed.)

Indian Architecture in Postcards

A New Perspective on a Modern Heritage

[transcript]

This publication was supported by funds from the Publication Fund for Open Access Monographs of the Federal State of Brandenburg, Germany.
Diese Veröffentlichung wurde aus Mitteln des Publikationsfonds für Open-Access-Monografien des Landes Brandenburg gefördert.

Bibliographic information published by the Deutsche Nationalbibliothek
The Deutsche Nationalbibliothek lists this publication in the Deutsche Nationalbibliografie; detailed bibliographic data are available in the Internet at http://dnb.d-nb.de

First published in 2023 by transcript Verlag, Bielefeld
© Éléonore Muhidine (ed.)

Cover layout: Maria Arndt, Bielefeld
Cover illustration: Private collection Muhidine, Berlin

https://doi.org/10.14361/9783839467169
Print-ISBN 978-3-8376-6716-5
PDF-ISBN 978-3-8394-6716-9
ISSN of series: 2702-8070
eISSN of series: 2702-8089

Focusing on a private collection of 60 postcards of modern architecture in Mumbai, New Delhi, Kolkata, Chennai and Agra, the contributors to this volume explore the many dimensions of modern architecture in India from the 1890s to the 1970s and share their own perspective on these objects. Experts on architectural history and visual studies, as well as postcard collectors provide new insights into a territory and its architectural heritage which is still largely unknown in Europe, and reflect on the postcard as a medium for historical research.

Contents

Architectural modernity in India
Sources and perspectives for research
An introduction

Éléonore Muhidine

This collection of architectural postcards and urban views of Indian metropolises between 1900 and 1970 was born out of the observation, by the European researcher that I am, of the acute lack of online visual sources for historians of architecture and 20th century cities who wish to immerse themselves in the architectural modernity of the Indian subcontinent. Despite the globalisation of exchanges between researchers and the stimulating perspectives offered by contemporary historical research—whether cross-cutting, comparative, connected or transnational—and despite the many projects for the digitisation of sources being carried out in parallel in Germany or the United States, India is still in the early stages of this process of digital preservation of archives, particularly with regard to making them available online. However, the threat posed by a general lack of interest in India's modern architectural heritage makes this need all the more pressing. This lack of interest is more marked than in Europe, for example, where initiatives for the documentation, preservation and transmission of this contemporary heritage are receiving some institutional attention, notably thanks to the activities of ICOMOS and of the DOCOMOMO chapters. But this historical and cultural heritage is also threatened by the tropical climate in some major urban centres—Mumbai and Kolkata—which has a direct impact on the conservation of the built environment and of the sources of architectural and urban history. Recent initiatives in several Indian metropolises include the creation of the Mumbai Art Deco Society Trust[1] and the Kolkata Immersive Trails research group[2] in 2016, two private research institutes that are working for the recognition—on a local scale and by individual rather than institutional actors –, transmission and preservation of the 20th century heritage of Indian cities.

Fig. 1: Marine Drive Boulevard: Bombay's waterfront in the 1970s.

Twentieth century architecture in India experienced several movements and experimented with important stylistic transitions, comparable to those that swept across Western countries, although in a time frame that lagged slightly behind French, German or British architecture, particularly before 1947. Art Deco, which developed in France, and particularly in Paris, between the wars,[3] flourished in Bombay and Calcutta around 1937–1947 at the dawn of Indian independence, while European countries were engaged in air warfare that led to massive de-

---

1   Art Deco Mumbai Trust (ADMT): https://www.artdecomumbai.com/ (02.02. 2023).

2   Kolkata Immersive Trails: https://de.immersivetrails.com/ (02.02.2023).

3   Bréon, Emmanuel (ed.), *Art déco France-Amérique du Nord*, Paris, Norma, 2022.

struction.[4] Similarly, hygienist functionalism and its idea of the garden city, expressed in the Paris region from the 1910s-1920s, thanks in particular to the commitment of Henri Sellier, saw various local interpretations towards the end of the 1930s. This is illustrated by the buildings on Marine Drive in Bombay, with their inner courtyards and large bay windows, all promising access to modern comfort in a city marked by squalor. The post-1947 period saw the spread of the international style, adopting the forms of inter-war modernism. The production and use of reinforced concrete in construction became systematic, supported by economic nationalisation: this is a feature of architectural production worldwide, also found in this region of Southeast Asia.[5] Major figures in modern Indian architecture emerged: Charles Correa (1930–2015), Balkrishna Vithaldas Doshi (1927–2023) and Raj Rewal (1934) succeeded in transforming this modernity, with its forms and theories largely imported from Europe and the United States, into a local architecture inspired by Indian traditions and adapted to climatic constraints.[6] The environmental thinking that accompanied Indian architecture of the 1960s and 1970s was a singular and innovative development at global level. In the 1970s, the political rapprochement with the USSR accompanied the birth of new architectural forms steeped in the socialist idea. The frescoes and glass mosaics that adorned public buildings during this period (postcard from the Calcutta cultural centre) reflect these cultural exchanges with the Eastern Bloc.

But 20th century Indian architecture is fascinating in that it shows a surprising (even disconcerting) capacity to absorb trends, beyond the Cold War ideological divides that entrapped the Western world. Thus,

---

4   Cohen, Jean-Louis, *Architecture in Uniform. Designing and Building for the Second World War*, New Haven, Yale University Press, 2011.

5   Stierli, Martino (ed.), *The Project of Independence. Architectures of Decolonization in South Asia 1947–1985*, MoMa, New York, 2022.

6   Mehrotra, Rahul (ed.), *World Architecture 1900–2000 A critical mosaic: South Asia*, New York, Springer, 2000. The projects reproduced in this book give an overview of the international modernity also taking hold in this part of the world.

post-modern ideas and, in particular, the principles of architectural citation and collage of references, can be found in certain urban projects of the 1970s. The Shalimar cinema (1979) in Bombay, with its film reels unrolled on the façade, is a striking example.[7] Taken as a whole, this architectural output (but also intellectual output, thanks to the publication of books and architectural magazines) constitutes a formidable terrain for the historian. Whether it be train and bus stations, cinemas, housing estates, foreign embassies, scientific research institutes, museums and art centres, or even international hotels, the forms and aspirations of the modern school of thought penetrated Indian territory from the beginning of the 20th century and attest to powerful exchanges and transfers between Europe, the United States and metropolitan India. This dynamic circulation of knowledge is driven by a dual flow of exchanges: those developed by architects and artists trained in the Western avant-garde and who chose, for economic, political or more personal reasons, to build closer ties with India (the esoteric movement took off in the enlightened circles of Germany in 1900 as part of the *Lebensreform* movement), and those initiated by the Indian cultural elites who trained in London, Berlin, Paris, New York or Chicago. The exchanges between the spirit of Weimar Germany and modernist Bombay were brought to light by the seminal works of historians such as Margit Franz,[8] Rachel Lee,[9] and Kris Manjapra.[10] This approach to Indian modernity through the prism of transfers between the West and India highlights exchanges

---

7   But architectural citation was already present before 1947, particularly in cinema architecture. See Jean-Louis Cohen's lecture on citation in architecture at the Collège de France on 3 March 2021 : Cohen, Jean-Louis, « Le travail de la citation en architecture et en urbanisme », URL : https://www.college-de-fran ce.fr/agenda/cours/formes-urbaines-en-mouvement-architecture-de-interur banite/le-travail-de-la-citation-en-architecture-et-urbanisme (02.02.2023).

8   Franz, Margit, *Gateway India: Deutschsprachiges Exil in Indien zwischen britischer Kolonialherrschaft, Maharadschas und Gandhi*, Graz, CLIO, 2015.

9   Lee, Rachel, *OK INDIA: Otto Königsberger, Urban Visions and Architecture in India*, University of Liverpool, TAG Press, 2015.

10   Manjapra, Kris, *Age of Entanglement: German and Indian Intellectuals across Empire*, Cambridge, Harvard historical studies, Harvard University Press, 2014.

that were long ignored by research. But cultural modernity also penetrated India through other transnational and interdisciplinary channels:
the Pathé film company, present in India since the early 20th century,[11]
contributed to the development of this new leisure activity and of the Indian film industry,[12] which today ranks first in the world, ahead of Holly-
wood. The impact of foreign industries was decisive in the introduction
of new urban practices and shapes. The presence of Italian lifts of the
Stigler company in most of the modern buildings—including the Eros
cinema palace (1938)—of Bombay in the 1920s and 1930s is a reminder of
this.

*Fig. 2: Eros Cinema (1938): an Art Deco-style monu-
ment built by Indian architects but furnished with lifts
from Stigler (Italy).*

While the enlightened Europe of the intellectuals and artists of the
1900s projected its fantasies of parallel worlds onto the ancient traditions of India and its spiritual movements, Western artistic modernity

---

11 Préval de, Jitka, *Camille Legrand. Un opérateur Pathé sur la route des Indes
1895–1920*, Paris, Riveneuve, 2021.

12 For an approach to the diversity of Indian cinema, see: Weil, Ophélie, *Bollywood
et les autres. Une histoire du cinéma* indien, Paris, Buchet Chastel, 2011; Rousseau,
Julien; Kessous, Hélène (eds.), *Bollywood Superstars - A Short Story of Indian Cinema*, Dijon, Les presses du Réel, 2022.

penetrated Indian territory via several channels (first through philan-thropists and the colonial administration[13] then, more individually, through social relations between Western and Indian intellectuals), Indian urban infrastructure was taking shape under the impact of un-bridled industrialisation—a reflection of a colonial system that led to the plundering of local resources.

On this point, we should bear in mind the context in which these build-ings were constructed, which no doubt explains the lack of interest in this built heritage. We recall Samia Henni's statement in the catalogue of the 2021 Venice Architecture Biennale, which reads: "Histories, the-ories, and practices of architecture and urbanism are intimately inter-related to processes of colonization. The world's territories and peo-ple have been constantly and continuously disturbed and marked by violent activities of war, occupation, exploitation, dispossession, de-struction, and construction. Since the fifteenth century, Western Euro-pean architects, both civil and military, have been actively participat-ing in constructing empires and framing their representations. These designers were commissioned to imagine and realize various infras-tructures, public buildings, and private settlements across the mul-tiple territories of the empires they worked for. The vastness and di-versity of colonial spaces around the world that resulted from these conditions have been instrumental in settling in the colonized land, exploiting, and transporting resources, and representing an unevenly distributed power [...] Stories of globalization are an extension of his-tories of colonization. An effort to understand architecture, its histo-ries and theories, as an integral part of the dynamic of the world's or-der and disorder rather than simply as a passive spectator and sup-plier of space, is fundamental. [...] Architecture operates on a planetary scale and depends on accumulated and distributed capital."[14]

---

13   Chopra, Preeti, *A Joint Enterprise. Indian Elites and the Making of British Bombay*, Minneapolis, University of Minnesota Press, 2011.

14   Essay by Henni, Samia, in: Sarkis, Hashim; Tannir, Ala (eds.), *Expansions. Re-sponses to How will we live together?*, Venice Architecture Biennale 2021; p. 95–96.

For applied arts, as for architecture, sources remain scattered between public institutions (Asiatic Society of Mumbai, National Archives of India, for example), private institutes (MARG Foundation, Mumbai; Charles Correa Foundation, Panaji/Goa) and isolated individual collectors that need to be identified through in-depth search via the abundant data available on social networks. This dispersion of sources is combined with a tropical climate that makes it difficult to preserve the originals. The political turbulence in 20th century India—notably the Independence of 1947, the partition of India with Pakistan, the military tensions in Kashmir with China in the 1950s and 1960s, and then the creation of Bangladesh (1971)—redrew the Indian national boundaries several times in the second half of the 20th century, disrupting the political and social order and impacting the preservation of historical sources. In this sense, a digitization of the archives is an emergency of primary importance for international historical research on India.[15]

Fig. 3: "Bombay: Souvenirs de passage" (Memories of a Journey) and the Hamidiya Masjid (1880).

---

15   What the ongoing DFG research project "MIDA Das Moderne Indien in Deutschen Archiven 1706–1989" (Zentrum Moderner Orient, Berlin) is highlighting. https://www.projekt-mida.de/ (02.02.2023).

The European research project Metromod[16] has addressed this need by presenting digitised archival material on its website and is contributing to future research on modern Bombay in the years 1910–1940. With the necessary modesty implied by the stance of the historian as much as by the reality of this collection, limited to just 60 postcards, this book project aspires to partially fill this gap through its contribution to this field of research.

The postcard as a tool for architectural and urban research

Despite the limitations of the postcard medium as a historical source, these 60 cards offer a relatively complete and original overview of the European view of India in the 20th century. The postcard as a medium for the dissemination of modern architecture is still more rarely used in research than other media such as architects' archives, specialised magazines, and the cultural press. However, while the postcard is an integral component of the cultural practices of its time and produces a discourse on the city and architectural modernity in the 20th century, it also permeates the architectural culture of architects. Examples include the controversial postcard taken from a photomontage showing the "Weißenhofsiedlung" of 1927, which crystallises the debates on architectural functionalism in the interwar period; the collection of 2,000 annotated postcards that Le Corbusier accumulated during his career (including postcards of the city of New Delhi, then under construction in the 1950s, and of the Jantar Mantar observatory in Jaipur),[17] or the use of postcards by Rem Koolhaas to illustrate his essay *Delirious New York* (1978). Their potential has also fascinated writers: among others,

---

16   METROMOD research project, LMU, Munich: https://metromod.net/project/ (02.02.2023).

17   The author thanks the archivist of the Le Corbusier Foundation, Arnaud Dercelles, for his valuable assistance. See also : Burriel Bielza, Luis, *Le Corbusier La passion des cartes*, Paris, Mardaga, 2013. On the postcard as an art history medium, see: Tillier, Bertrand, "The Postcard, a Documentary Multiple of the Masterpiece", *Perspective*, 2019/2; p. 239–48.

Georges Perec (series of texts entitled "243 real colour postcards", 1978) and Jacques Derrida with his satirical essay *The Post Card. From Socrates to Freud and Beyond* (1980). As symbols of imagery for the masses, products of a commercial strategy, postcards form an invaluable visual resource. And when they represent urban views or specific buildings, they actively train the viewer's eye and nurture the culture of architectural travel. While they reflect a vision—necessarily idealised, that being their primary function—of a building or a city (we send a postcard to tell our loved ones about a pleasantly exotic trip, generally reserving any accounts of bad experiences for our return), photographs attest to a given moment, a moment captured in the history of a building or the urbanisation of a metropolis and provide an archive of the city.

Fig. 4: Mumbai, View from Malabar Hill in the 1970s.

Postcards do not reflect the real state of the architecture, they do not give any information on the preparatory phase of the project, nor on the construction phase and the difficulties encountered. These photographs, designed to advertise a building or a city, highlight their aesthetic qualities (undeniable qualities for the *flâneur*), capture an ultimately fleeting moment in the history of an urban architecture. They celebrate the moment of the photographic shot rather than providing precise historical information to reconstruct a necessarily more complex architectural his-

tory, involving economic, political, and cultural reflections and a plunge
into the controversies of an era. Thus, the postcard as a medium fits in
with Siegfried Kracauer's definition of photography when he wrote: "Under the photograph of a human being, his history lies buried as under a
blanket of snow."[18]

But viewed from the perspective of the architectural culture of an
era, a culture of the people rather than the elite, these postcards allow us
to trace the series of famous buildings that marked their time. Viewed
in this light, these postcards provide a visual chronicle of a collective
view of architecture, a chronicle captured in the present moment, not
in the historian's reconstructed time. Far from the disturbing views of
French seminarians teaching the language of the coloniser to the children of Pondicherry, or the countless views of the Taj Mahal mausoleum
in Agra or the Mughal Fort in Old Delhi, these postcards have the common denominator of making 20th century architecture their central motif. It would undoubtedly be necessary to explore the companies that specialised in the production, printing and distribution of postcards in the
colonial context, and to question the alliances underpinning this highly
lucrative industry, especially since, in the case of these Indian cards, it
is not unusual to find the words "Printed in Germany" on the back. Photographed in Bombay or Calcutta by professionals whose equipment was
manufactured and imported from the West, then sometimes printed in
Europe before being sent back to India where they were bought by travellers who in turn sent them to their families in Europe, these cards seem
to have travelled further than their writers. Printed in series of millions
of copies, the postcard embodies economic capitalism and the globalisation of trade, but also the democratisation of travel in the 20th century, previously the preserve of the privileged social classes to which the
great explorers belonged (Alexander von Humboldt, Alexandra David-
Neel, Paul-Emile Victor, for example). It is undoubtedly the mercantile
and popular side of the picture postcard that led architectural historians to lose interest in them. However, the architectural postcard calls for

18   Kracauer, Siegfried, "Photography", in: *L'Ornement de la masse. Essais sur la moder-
nite weimarienne* (1963), Paris, La Découverte, 2008; p.39.

a critical analysis wherein lies its scientific value, as the historian Igor Marjanovic points out: "Postcard collections remove objects from their original context of consumer tourism into a world of subjective spatial and temporal narrative, replacing everyday consumption with the production of history."[19]

An original feature of this book is that it brings together authors who, in some cases, have an in-depth knowledge of the Indian terrain in its current state. Their texts reflect a profound gulf between the idealised urban visions of postcards and the reality of Indian megacities today.[20] As a collective work that aims to build bridges between the different disciplines and communities of researchers represented (art history,[21] architecture,[22] economics,[23] media sociology,[24] heritage studies[25]), this book intends to contribute to the scientific discussion on certain aspects of architectural modernity in India, rather than to provide a complete overview. It is guided by the desire to raise the profile of this rich Indian heritage in the humanities and in the history of architecture over the long 20th century. However, the postcard approach provides only a tiny glimpse into the possibilities open to a necessarily collective, preferably international, research undertaking, which will need to con-

---

19   Marjanovic, Igor, "Postcards and the Making of Architectural History", 92nd ACSA Annual Meeting, 18–21.03.2004, https://www.acsa-arch.org/chapter/po stcards-and-the-making-of-architectural-history-the-case-of-the-alvin-boyar sky-and-rem-koolhaas/ (02.02.2023).

20   Bansal, Anupam, "Delhi Beyond its appearance".

21   Khan, Omar, "Building Postcards: Rössler's Calcutta 1896".

22   Sanyal, Saptarshi, "Framing Fragments. The Image, Modernity, and Architecture"; Muhidine, Eléonore, "The Taj Mahal Hotel, Imperial, Sun'n'Sand, Oberoi, and others: the Indian chapter of the 20th-century grand hotel".

23   Rault-Chodankar, Yves-Marie, "Before take-off: waiting for India's globalization at the Sahar International Airport in 1974".

24   Kaden, Ben, "Image, recto, verso, context. Approaching Deltiology as a method".

25   Chopra, Preeti, "Greetings from Bombay! Pictures of Colonial Complexity"; Bhatawadekar, Shraddha, "Transport and Communication as Symbols of Modernity in India: A Cultural Perspective".

front the problems of rapidly deteriorating physical sources and their geographical dispersion.

Modern architecture in India: a history of transfer over the long 20th century

Indian architectural modernity is complex and hybrid; its history has been shaped by national turning points and transnational transfers. This modernity is taken on board over the long 20th century and is nurtured by foreign influences that are imposed, but also projected and desired, by certain local backers. Indeed, while the colonial context imposed certain trends, notably a neo-Gothic style in the public buildings of Bombay 1880 (a style that can be found in London buildings of the same period[26]), openness to international trends claiming a simplicity of form and means—was also very marked within enlightened circles.

Fig. 5: Visweswaraiah Industrial and Technological Museum, Bangalore, 1962, architect: unknown.

---

26   The similarities between the buildings of Farrington Road in London and those of the Fort district of Bombay are spectacular. The gothic revival fashion, of which Viollet-le-Duc was the spokesman in France and John Ruskin the theorist in England, was thus exported to the colonized countries, without any prior reflection on the specificities of the climate and its impact on architecture.

After 1947, the Indian architectural community was confronted with the need to define a modern aesthetic that was specifically Indian, marked by a reflection on function rather than on form. This gave rise, in the 1960s, to a school of environmental and sustainable architectural thought that was ahead of its time, and notably represented by the projects ofBalkrishna Doshi (School of Architecture, CEPT, Ahmedabad, 1966–68) or of Laurie Baker (Loyola Graduate Women's Hostel, Trivandum, 1970).

In architecture, India received large projects that were sometimes modern, sometimes borne by a modernising ideal,[27] and which were to have an impact on the scale of the continent and of neighbouring countries, while also broadening the architectural vocabulary of smaller projects on a regional scale. The case of cinemas is still exemplary in this sense: the Bombay 1940 cinema palaces, designed to accommodate more than 3,000 people, were reproduced in series and on a smaller scale in the secondary towns of Maharashtra. In Calcutta, the same phenomenon occurred for the cinemas of Bengal, and in Delhi, for those of Uttar Pradesh. India is a complex territory, marked by modern projects that belong to a global history of modernity, involving major figures: Eckart Muthesius in Indore,[28] Otto Königsberger in Mysore and Bangalore, Le Corbusier in Ahmedabad and Chandigarh,[29] Balkrishna Vithaldas Doshi in Ahmedabad, Raj Rewal[30] in New Delhi, Charles Correa in Bombay, New Delhi and Kolkata. Less well known is the in-

---

27   Stephens, Robert, *Bombay Imagined: An Illustrated History of the Unbuilt City*, Mumbai, Urbsindis, 2022.

28   Niggl, Reto, *Eckart Muthesius. Der Palast des Maharadschas in Indore. Architektur und Interieur*, Stuttgart, Arnold, 1996.

29   Moos, Stanislaus von, *Chandigarh 1956*, Zürich, Scheidegger & Spies, 2010; Högner, Bärbel, *Chandigarh nach Le Corbusier. Ethnografie einer postkolonialen Planstadt in Indien*, Berlin, Reimer, 2016.

30   Gill, Sandrine, *Raj Rewal, From Architecture to Cultural Landscape*, Marseille, Parenthèses, 2020.

volvement of Frei Otto in Ahmedabad in the 1970s (Prototype tent project for climate refugees).[31]

Beyond building projects, the European influence is reflected in Indian architectural journals, in particular in the magazine *MARG*[32] (founded in 1946) and in the *Journal of the Indian Institute of Architecture*, both published in Bombay. Theoretical texts by Erich Mendelsohn, Patrick Geddes, Andrew Boyd (a British architect who contributed to the spread of modernism in Ceylon in the 1940s)[33] were published in *MARG* under the impetus of progressive intellectuals, such as the writer and art critic Mulk Raj Anand (1905–2004), and Indian architects receptive to the idea of modernity as a project for reforming society.[34] Unquestionably, there are strong links between modern architectural thinking and the garden cities of England, the German art schools (Darmstadt, Bauhaus) and theatres (Piscator's theatre) of the avant-garde, the cinema palaces of Paris 1930 (the Grand Rex), and the modernist architecture of Bombay 1930–1940. The innovative character of this urban Indian modernity lies in a synthesis between functionalism, Art déco and traditional Indian decorative motifs. The bas-reliefs of the New India Assurance Building (1936), showing stylised Indian workers, are a major example. In Calcutta as in New Delhi, European influences, and resonances with the modern cultural metropolises of London, Paris, and Berlin[35] can also be retraced. Numerous studies have shown that architectural magazines, the main medium for reproduction of architectural images, were widely circulated during the 20th century. This was also the case in India, and

---

31   The author would like to thank the archivist of the Frei Otto Archive, Martin Kunz, for his advice. (SAAI-Archive, KIT, Karlsruhe, Germany).

32   Lee, Rachel; James-Chakraborty, Kathleen, "Marg Magazine: A Tryst with Architectural Modernity", *ABE Journal*, 2012, http://journals.openedition.org/abe/62 3 (02.02.2023).

33   Dalvi, Mustansir (ed.), *20th Century Compulsions. Modern Indian Architecture from the Marg Archives*, Mumbai, Marg Foundation, 2016.

34   Notably Balkrishna V. Doshi, Durga Bajpai, Charles Correa.

35   Cohen, Jean-Louis, Cycle at the Collège de France, Paris, "Formes urbaines en mouvement: l'architecture de l'interurbanité", 2021.

circulation may even have been boosted by the British colonial presence in architecture schools and their university libraries.[36]

The collection (based, of course, on the limited resources available) comprises a total of 60 postcards, 41 in colour, representing the diversity of architectural forms in India between 1880 and 1970. Before we present it in more detail, it should be stressed that a collection is the fruit of several elements of chance: that of the search, fruitful or otherwise, of the choices made, necessarily subjective, and of the budget allocated to its expansion. The subjects represented reflect the places visited by Europeans travelling in India between the 1910s and 1980s, and not the centres of modern architecture in India. Thus, Ahmedabad, Madras, Lucknow and Chandigarh, which deserve to be included in this collection, are absent because no postcards of these cities sent to Europe could be found. In this sense, the collection presented is fragmentary. But this is a constant dimension of this project of collected essays and resonates with a definition of 20th century modernity and its spatial reproduction via an almost infinite range of major projects and secondary realisations.

The subjects have been deliberately chosen to represent the richness of this 20th century heritage. They are essentially photographs (with the exception of a model of the Taj Mahal Hotel and its counterpart, the Taj Mahal Tower) which can be classified under 6 thematic categories:

Communication and urban development

- Floral Fountain, Mumbai, 1864, architect Richard Norman Shaw (Fig.18; 24; 29; 32)
- Old pontoon Bridge, Kolkata (Fig.14)
- Victoria Station, Mumbai, 1888, architect Frederick William Stevens (Fig.21; 31)
- General Post Office, Mumbai, 1913, architect John Begg (Fig.30)
- New Railway Station, Howrah (Fig.33)

---

36 Here, the involvement of the British architect, educator and author Claude Batley between 1923 and 1943 at the J. J. School of Architecture in Bombay should be mentioned (*Bombay's Houses and Homes*, 1949).

- Western Railway Office, Mumbai (Fig.35)
- Kennedy Sea-Face, Mumbai, 1920, planner unknown (Fig.17)
- View of Churchgate, Mumbai, 1940s, author unknown (Fig.56)
- Connaught Place, New Delhi, 1931, architect Robert Tor Russell (Fig.25)
- New Telephone Exchange, Kolkata, date and architect unknown (Fig.34)
- Hornby Road, Mumbai (Fig.40)
- Urban view around Churchgate, Mumbai (Fig.47)
- Marine Drive Promenade, Mumbai, 1930–1940;[37] several views including Kapur Mahal, Zaver Mahal, Keval Mahal and Soona Mahal (Fig.1; 55; 46; 49)
- Airport Terminal, Mumbai, Santacruz Building, 1948, architect unknown (Fig.36; 37)
- Brabourne Road, Kolkata (Tea Board India, 1954, architect unknown) (Fig.57)
- Mumbai suburbs, 1960s, large housing estates, architect unknown (Fig.38)

Economy

- Crawford Market, Mumbai, 1869, architect William Emerson (Fig.19)
- Petroleum House (Esso-Building), Mumbai, 1954, architect unknown (Fig.48)
- View of the Port, Panaji (Goa) in the 1960s (Fig.7)

Luxury hotels

- Taj Mahal, Mumbai, 1903, architects DN Mirza and Sitaram Khanderao Vaidya (565 rooms, 42 suites, 11 restaurants) (Fig.22)
- The Imperial, New Delhi, 1936, architect F. B. Blomfield and Edwin Lutyens (225 rooms, 44 suites, 6 restaurants, 2 bars) (Fig.44)

---

37   This seafront avenue has an exceptional heritage and was added to the list of UNESCO world heritage sites in 2018.

- Clarks Shiraz, Agra, 1950s (Fig.60)
- The Ashok Hotel, New Delhi, 1956, architect E. B. Doctor (550 rooms) (Fig.41)
- Claridge's Hotel, New Delhi, 1955, architect unknown (Fig.61)
- Oberoi Inter Continental, New Delhi, 1965 (many foreign designers, including the American Joseph Grusczak, Irene D'Alessio, 350 rooms) (Fig.40; 43)
- Sun'n'Sand, Juhu Beach, Mumbai, 1962, architect unknown (Fig.42)
- Taj Mahal Tower, Mumbai, 1972, architect Melton Bekker, decorator Dale Keller (Fig.23)

Cultural spaces

- Kali Temple, Kolkata (Fig.9)
- 19th century hotel, Old Delhi (Fig.45)
- Hamidiya Masjid, Mumbai (Fig.3)
- Eros Cinema, Mumbai, 1938, architect Sorabji K. Bhedwar, decorator Fritz von Drieberg (Fig.2)
- View of Malabar Hill, Mumbai, 1970s (Fig.4; 39)
- All Air India, Radio House, New Delhi, 1940, architect unknown (Fig.27)
- Jehangir Art Gallery, Mumbai, 1952, architect Durga Bajpai (Fig.8)
- Rabindra Sadan, Kolkata, 1961, architect unknown (Fig.6)
- Visweswaraiah Industrial and Technological Museum, Bangalore, 1962, architect unknown (Fig.5)

Places of power

- Parliament House, New Delhi, 1927, architects Edwin Lutyens und Herbert Baker (Fig.26)
- National Physical Laboratory, New Delhi, 1950, architect unknown (Fig.53)
- German Embassy, New Delhi, 1962, architect Johannes Krahn (Fig.51)

Places of Modern Indian Memory

- Black Hole Memorial, Kolkata, 1901 (Fig.13)
- Mahatma Gandhi Memorial, Sanjay Gandhi National Park, Mumbai, 1969 (Fig.58)
- Valluvar Kottam (memorial to the poet Saint Thiruvalluvar), Chennai, 1976, architect V. Ganapati Sthapati (Fig.59)

Modern India through the eyes of European intellectuals

The backs of these postcards convey a wide variety of travel impressions, fragmentary messages, sometimes cryptic, often quite mundane. This section aims to compare these anonymous writings with those of famous European artists whose literary or cinematographic work was nurtured by their experiences and discoveries during their travels to India. The French intellectual André Malraux (1901–1976) met Jawaharlal Nehru for the first time in Switzerland in January 1936, after discovering India in 1930 on a private trip. Other visits followed, in 1958, 1965, 1973 and finally 1974. India was his last trip abroad, before his death in 1976. Despite this passion for India, reflected in his political engagement and in his essay, *Le Musée Imaginaire* (1947),[38] a seminal work in the history of art, Malraux never wrote a novel about India. In this essay, he quotes and reproduces photographs of sculptures from the caves of Elephanta, Ellora and Ajanta, creating parallels with the monumental Mexican sculpture of Teotihuacan, the Egyptian pyramids and Buddhist sculptures in China. With visionary genius, he proposes a world history of sculpted art, and invites the reader-viewer to compare these ancient works beyond their regional context alone. But Malraux's India is also one of cultural action deeply rooted in the modernisation of India in the 1950s. His internationalist spirit found affinities with Nehru's political project, and the two men met regularly in Paris (1936, 1960, 1961) and New Delhi (1958).

---

38   Grasskamp, Walter, *André Malraux und das imaginäre Museum. Die Weltkunst im Salon*, Berlin, C. H. Beck, 2014; p. 232.

In a letter to Charles de Gaulle on 13 November 1958, he described his programme for the coming weeks:

"Then I would like to visit, not the universities of today, but rather the great centres of art or thought which, in India, play the role of our medieval universities: the Institutes of Indian Culture in Bangalore and Bombay, the Institute of Oriental Research in Poona, the Music Academy in Madras, the Bose Institute, Sanskrit College in Benares, etc. In each of these cities, I would gladly receive a number of visitors. (No doubt it would be agreeable to visit the new capital of Indian Punjab, Chandigarh, built by Le Corbusier and dominated by the 'Open Hand')".[39]

These words resonate with the collection presented here, which includes a physics research institute in New Delhi and a cultural centre in Kolkata. The cultural links between 1950s France and independent India were strong, with the great Chandigarh construction project headed by Le Corbusier (a Swiss who took French nationality in 1930) being the most important example.

Fig. 6: Kolkata, Rabindra Sadan Cultural Centre (1967).

---

39   Perrier, Jean-Claude (ed.), *André Malraux et la Tentation de l'Inde*, Paris, Galli-
      mard, 2004; p. 182.

A few years after the "Art Treasures of India" exhibition at the Petit Palais in Paris (1960) organised by André Malraux, it was the French filmmaker Louis Malle (1932–1995) who discovered Indian culture in 1968, when he was only 26 years old. Interviewing European travellers on the mythical "hippie trail", Malle recounts in his *Travel Diaries* their astonishment at this "initiatory journey" (an astonishment he shared), the dream of a whole generation of Westerners. His impressions of these travellers, who appear to be profoundly out of touch with Indian reality, shed light on some of the texts on the back of postcards sent in the 1970s:

> "They live completely on the fringes of the countries they travel through, which puts them at the total mercy of the authorities and the people of each country. They tell stories of prison, beating, rape, they are charming with their Parisian accents, incredibly first-hand. [...] They talk about love, war, the West, money, communism. [...] They are nineteen years old. One of them is exempted from military service, but the other refuses to report for duty. [...] They claim to be Fourierists, they want to set up a phalanstery, to abolish money." [40]

Louis Malle went to India to make a series of documentary films (*L'Inde fantôme: Réflexions sur un voyage*, a series of seven documentaries for television broadcast in 1969, and a film, *Calcutta*), capturing scenes of daily life in the India that fascinated him. "For the rest of his life, India was really an immense ghost that never stopped haunting him. He often spoke to me about it, he looked at pictures, he asked me about it, as if it were a dream he had accidentally entered at a certain point in his life, and from which he could not detach himself", wrote his friend, the film director Jean-Claude Carrière, on this subject. [41] For *Calcutta*, Malle filmed the ghats—the staircases that descend into the sacred Ganges River—the Howrah Bridge (also shown on one of the cards in the collection), the second-hand book sellers on College Street, the stalls manned by sculptors carving statues of deities in the alleys of Kumortuli. Taking a sociological

---

40   Malle, Louis, *L'Inde fantôme. Carnet de voyage (1967–1968)*, Paris, Gallimard, 2005; p. 167.

41   Ibid; p. 7.

look at the capital of Bengal, Louis Malle's film offers a beginner's guide to life in Calcutta, showing street scenes that are like emblems of political, economic, cultural and religious facts. For the series of television films, he shot a scene during a public education session of the Madras family planning centre (an episode that echoes a stamp, found on many of the cards, representing "Family Planning" in 1976), followed by a scene depicting a handout of Soviet-made condoms, a reminder of the political links between 1970s India and the Soviet bloc. His more personal recollections, collected in travel diaries published after his death, are evocative of the texts of some of the postcards in the collection:

> "This morning I am writing on the terrace of the hotel in Gopalpur, it is 6.30 a.m., the sun is still very low. In front of me, the beach, the water, the fishermen bringing in their nets, the very soft, slightly funereal light of tropical mornings. I feel an incredible rush of nostalgia [...]. Seeing this boat struggle against the waves, I feel a strange impression, which, if I analyse it, combines both the obvious feeling of the beauty of nature and its total harmony with this group of men, to which I add a whole potential of emotions comprising both my past memories and my dreams, the same dreams that I have had since my first journeys, and which have impelled me to make this one [...]. It is precisely when travelling that you find your bearings, that your character takes his place more clearly, in relation to beings and situations with which the contrast is sharper than at home. I travel to escape my character as a little Frenchman, and it is the journey that makes it perceptible to me."[42]

Finally, the Italian writer Antonio Tabucchi (1943–2012) discovered India in the 1980s. This journey and these discoveries gave rise to a short novel, *Indian Nocturne*, a story full of mystery and which inspired Alain Corneau to make a film, in equally twilight tones, in 1989. In this novel, more like a long hallucination, the narrator goes in search of an old friend who has disappeared and who is none other than himself.

---

42   Ibid.; p. 168–69.

Fig. 7: Panaji (Goa), View of the port, 1970s.

This search takes him to places as eclectic as the Taj Mahal Hotel in Bombay, to slum hotels in a dilapidated "Cage District [which] was much worse than I had imagined. I'd seen it in the photographs of a famous photographer and thought I was prepared for human misery, but photographs enclose the visible in a rectangle. The visible without a frame is always something else."[43] We also discover the setting of a hospital in which the narrator talks to a doctor, then a mysterious Theosophical Society in the state of Goa, and finally a bus-stop on the Madras-Mangalore Road, a bus station depicted in a night scene ("The night was soft and damp with a strong scent of herbs. I took a turn round the bus, smoked a cigarette leaning on the steps at the back, and then headed for the waiting-room. On the door jamb someone had stuck a picture of a divinity unknown to me, done in coloured chalk").[44] It is both a realistic and mysterious vision of the traveller's India that unfolds in this novel. The first scene, set in a taxi along Marine Drive, illustrates some of the maps in the collection which show several views of this mythical boulevard bordering the Arabian Sea and featured in many Hindi films. The last chapter of this short, yet extremely rich novel features a mailman character

---

43   Tabucchi, Antonio, *Indian Nocturne*, Edinburgh, Canongate Books, 1984; p. 3–4.
44   Ibid.; p. 62–63.

who seems to enter into a direct dialogue with this collection. His cryptic words resonate, once again, with this collection. Tabucchi's mailman seems almost to be talking to the collector when he confides to the narrator on a beach in the state of Goa:

> "I worked as a mailman in Philadelphia, at eighteen already walking the streets with my bag over my shoulder, without fail, every morning, in summer when the tar turns to molasses and in winter when you slip on the city snow. For ten years, carrying letters. You don't know how many letters I've carried, thousands and thousands. They were all upper class, rich, the people on the envelopes. Letters from all around the world: Miami, Paris, London, Caracas".[45] The narrator then asks him, "And what are you doing today? His surprising answer is clear: "I write postcards. It's me who writes the ladies and gents of Philadelphia now. Postcards with a nice sea and the deserted Calangute Beach, and on the back I write best wishes from mailman Tommy".[46]

In conclusion, we have chosen to reproduce three handwritten texts from the corpus that stand out for their originality. They reflect powerful emotions felt during a journey, or more concrete experiences, preserved only through the medium of the postcard. We felt that they deserved to appear, at the end of this introduction, in a collective work that aims to capture the diversity of possible views on India and its metropolises in the 20th century, on modernity in architecture and on the postcard as a medium of modern architectural culture.

> 9 August 1965
> "Dear friends,
> When I arrived here, I wanted to come and chat with you and tell you about my trip. But the damn old sun sucked the little energy I had left after two weeks of amoebic dysentery where I thought I would collapse. Now it's too late, I'll have to tell you in person when I get back. The violent monsoon rains seem to have subsided, but the sky

---

45   Ibid.; p. 83.
46   Ibid.; p. 87.

is leaden. The heat is so heavy, so humid that you only have to take three steps outside to come home dripping sweat. We are in a real hole, clustered around the industrial complex: coal mine, aluminium factory and rolling mills, all in a flat country in the middle of rice fields. Everything is exuberant: bugs of all kinds and sizes (especially rats, cockroaches, and ants), the scent of flowers (I've never seen so many species of jasmine!), the misery of human masses beyond our European imagination. No meat, no wine, no whisky, and no car. And yet the morale is good. Sometimes we dream of a holiday in the snow. Have a good trip and be assured of our warmest sympathy. Monique"
Sent to France

10 May 1975
"My darling, I still have not received any letter from you. Should I come back or not? I would like to return, of course. Here it is... No fun at all. Please write quickly."
Sent to Germany (West-Germany, West-Berlin)

1975 (stamp date)
"Many warm greetings from beautiful Bombay from your Roland. Yesterday is 33 degrees as it is for us during summer. Maybe you have seen me in the "Current Camera"? I hope so. See you soon!" Sent to Germany (East-Germany, Hoyerswerda)

References

Burriel Bielza, Luis, *Le Corbusier La Passion des cartes*, Paris, Mardaga, 2013.

Ching, Francis D. K.; Jarzombek, Mark M.; Prakash, Vikramaditya (eds.), *A Global History of Architecture*, Hoboken, John Wiley and Sons, 2006.

Chopra, Preeti, *A Joint Enterprise: Indian Elites and the Making of British Bombay*, Minneapolis, University of Minnesota Press, 2011.

Cohen, Jean-Louis, *The Future of Architecture since 1889. A Worldwide History*, New York, Phaidon Press, 2012.

Correa, Charles, *A Place in the Shade. The New Landscape and other essays*, Ostfildern, Hatje Cantz, 2012.

Franz, Margit, *Gateway India—Deutschsprachiges Exil in Indien zwischen britischer Kolonialherrschaft, Maharadschas und Gandhi*, Graz, CLIO, 2015.

Grasskamp, Walter, *André Malraux und das imaginäre Museum. Die Weltkunst im Salon*, Berlin, C. H. Beck, 2014.

Geary, Christaud M.; Webb, Virginie-Lee (eds.), *Delivering Views. Distant Cultures in Early Postcards*, New York, Smithsonian Institution Scholary Press, 1998.

Gill, Sandrine, *Raj Rewal. De l'architecture au paysage culturel*, Marseille, Parenthèses, 2020.

Malle, Louis, *L'Inde fantôme. Carnet de voyage*, Paris, Gallimard, 2005.

Manjapra, Kris, *Age of Entanglement. German and Indian Intellectuals across Empire*, Cambridge, Harvard University Press, 2014.

Mehrotra, Rahul; Dwivedi, Sharada, *Bombay the Cities within*, Mumbai, Eminence, 2001.

Mehrotra, Rahul (ed.), *World Architecture. A Critical Mosaic 1900–2000. Volume VIII, South Asia*, New York, Springer, 2000.

Moos, Stanislaus von (ed.), *Chandigarh 1956*, Zürich, Scheidegger Spiess, 2010.

Niggel, Reto (ed.), *Eckart Muthesius 1930. Indien 1930–1939. Architektur, Design, Fotografie*, Munich, Goethe-Institut, 1999.

Perrier, Jean-Claude (ed.), *André Malraux et la Tentation de l'Inde*, Paris, Gallimard, 2004.

Préval de, Jitka, *Camille Legrand. Opérateur Pathé sur la route des Indes*, Paris, Riveneuve, 2021.

Sarkis, Hashim; Tannir, Ala (eds.), *EXPANSIONS. How will we live together? Biennale architettura 2021*, Milano, Silvana Editoriale, 2021.

Stephens, Robert, *Bombay imagined: An Illustrated History of the Unbuilt City*, Mumbai, Urbs Indis, 2022.

Stierli, Martino; Pieris, Anoma; Anderson, Sean (eds.), *The Project of Independence. Architectures of Decolonization in South Asia 1947–1985*, New York, MoMA, 2022.

Tabucchi, Antonio, *Indian Nocturne*, Edinburgh, Canongate Books, 1984.

Tillier, Bertrand, "The Postcard, a Documentary Multiple of the Masterpiece", *Perspective*, 2019/2.

*Fig. 8: Mumbai, The Jehangir Art Gallery (1952) with, in the
background, the CST Museum (formerly called Prince of Wales
Museum, 1905).*

Building Postcards: Rössler's Calcutta 1896

Omar Khan

Fig. 9: *This colorized photograph of the Kali temple in Calcutta (now Kolkata) shows a street scene around 1890.*

One can reasonably argue that the best postcards were the first post-cards. Wafer-thin rectangles that fell out from multiple stone pressings, court-sized lithographic postcards are today considered among the finest exemplars of the craft for their rarity, rich colors and elaborate designs. They appeared in Alpine hamlets and mountain villages in Germany, Austria and Switzerland in the early 1890s, became popular in those countries by 1895, and then spread through the world like an "infesting microbe."[1]

---

1   Perry, Katharine, "Tirade à La Carte," *Putnam's*, 3:336, reprinted in Postcardy.com.

It is the relationships between images suggested by these multi-view "Greetings from" cards that make them most interesting, the dynamics on a tiny space intentionally designed to be iconic, a loaded object calling attention to itself. Competitive cost and price pressures grew with the product's sudden popularity. International treaties, ships and trains, the need to be brief as time seemed to speed up, all combined to make the postcard the first global image communications platform by 1900. Market pressures led publishers to reach for less expensive production alternatives like the collotype, halftone, and real photograph postcard. The cost of the "poor man's phantasm"[2] became critical once they started to flood the market. The colored lithographic multi-view card was driven underground almost as soon as it emerged. Something was lost in the transition. The quick switch from lithographs to collotypes and halftones accompanied the move of written messages from front to the back of postcards in Europe around 1902. It simplified the press, facilitating the quick-to-print single view card. One picture became one postcard. These were usually made from photographs, similar to the pretty little boxed views in lithographic cards had sprung from. But early lithographic postcards left about a third or quarter of the space on the front blank for the sender to write on by hand, add a personal mark or stamp, setting up another relationship between image and text, visual meaning and inky materiality. If no message or mark was added, images wrapped in designs with shimmering borders stood out against the creamy emptiness.

The Calcutta series by W. Rössler

W. Rössler's six "Calcutta" postcard set from 1896 is probably the very first of its kind in British India. They appeared just as similar cards had become common in cities like Vienna, Frankfurt, Budapest and Berlin.

---

2   Alloula, Malek, *The Colonial Harem*, Minneapolis, University of Minnesota Press, 1986; p. 4.

Rössler's cards offer a novel way to explore the myths and physical structures of the Raj. For the problem of the building architect was the same as that of the postcard artist and publisher: how to fill a space, whether two or three dimensional. Rössler's Calcutta series shows how buildings, people and icons fit into the battle for space between East and West in early lithographic cards.

Fig. 10: W. Rössler's six "Calcutta" postcard set from 1896. Collection Omar Khan.

What Christopher Pinney calls a "common epistemological space"[3] is formed on these dramatic little stages that branded the capital of the Empire's richest province, Bengal. One sender of a card below (*Nautch Girl*) called it "My dears, a little picture [*Bildchen*] of Calcutta."[4] Perhaps these cards are like proto-movies (the dancing girl aside), moving from scene to scene, except that it is the eye of the viewer not the cut of the director that decides when.

Fig. 11: "Nautch Girl", Omar Khan Collection.

William Rössler was an Austrian photographer, probably born in what is now Czech Bohemia, in 1864. He came to India in 1888.[5] He is said to have joined the old and leading photography studio in the city, Johnston & Hoffmann at 22 Chowringhee road, in the heart of

---

3   Pinney, Christopher, *The Coming of Photography to India*, London, The British Library, 2008; p. 114.

4   Mathur Collection, *Nautch Girl*, postally used in Calcutta Dec. 8, 1900. The German "Ihr Lieben, ein Bildchen von Calcutta."

5   W. Rössler first appears in *Thacker's Indian Directory* entries for Calcutta in 1900, and in most subsequent years until 1915 with premises at 30 Creek Row. He does not appear in earlier *Thacker's* as an independent operator.

the colonial shopping area in 1890.[6] His profession is given as artist in the Certificate of Marriage from October 31st, 1894 between William and Priscilla Louise Wintgens ("Louisa"), under the heading "British Subject." She was a widow, the daughter of a deceased Superintendent of Police, he a bachelor. She was previously married to Adolphus Edward Wintgens, then himself a widower in 1888 (cemeteries were busy for colonists in old Calcutta).[7] In *Thacker's Indian Directory 1897* Rössler is listed as an assistant at Bourne & Shepherd's studio at 8 Chowringhee road.[8] This is interesting because *Thacker's* entries refer to the year before they were published, when the information was collected.

Given that the first Rössler Calcutta postcard is postmarked in 1896[9] (Fig. 1, *Native Ayah*), their publication may have been an entrepreneurial effort preceding the setting up of his very own studio. In the 1900 edition "W. Roessler, Photographer, 30, Creek Row," is listed for the first time in *Thacker's*, among a dozen or so major city photographers, which would make his independent business as a photographer having started

---

6   Letter to the India Office dated 6 Oct. 1914 by W Rössler. IOR-L-PJ-6-1343.

7   Certificate of Marriage between between William Rössler and Priscilla Louise Wintgens, Oct. 31, 1894, Registrar General of Births, Deaths and Marriages, Bengal. Louise Wintgens (then Strettell) was also listed as a widow when she married Gustave Adolph Wintgens June 1, 1888, Register of Marriages at St. James Church, Calcutta. All these records were seen at FindMyPast.com, (02.02.2023). Archive references Z/N/11/8/304 and N-1-204/149 respectively.

8   *Thacker's Indian Directory 1897*, Calcutta, Thacker, Spink & Co.; p. 3526. He is also listed as a Resident living at 29 Convent Road, Entally [Calcutta]. Bourne & Shepherd had nine named European assistants at studios in Calcutta, Bombay and Simla that year, and for photographic assistants to bounce from firm to firm was common.

9   Mathur Collection dated Dec. 1, 1896 and postmarked in Calcutta, December 2, 1896.

in 1899.[10] He will continue to appear at 30 Creek Row through the 1915 edition of *Thacker's*.[11]

Interferences and cultural transfers between India and Europe around 1900

Germans and Austrians were welcomed by Indians. There were many such photographers working in India at the time, including Thomas Paar, another Austrian who had a studio in Darjeeling, the Himalayan hill station frequented by Calcutta's elite and tourists in the summer (Paar was also an early postcard publisher).[12] The freedom movement was beginning to get traction (the Congress Party had been formed in 1885). Bengal would soon be rocked by the Swadeshi ("self-rule") movement among educated and middle-class Bengalis undergoing an intellectual and political renaissance that would bring the city's Rabindranath Tagore the first Nobel Prize awarded to an Indian in 1913. In the words of the fine chronicler of the city, Krishna Dutta, "during the second half of the nineteenth century...beneath the surface there was a gradual deterioration of the relationship between the rulers and the ruled."[13]

We know from Fritz Schleicher, the German entrepreneur and manager of the pioneering Ravi Varma Press in Bombay, the first publisher of postcards printed in India in 1898, who told a German paper magazine

---

10   He is listed in *Thacker's Indian Directory*, Calcutta, Thacker, Spink & Co., 1900; p. 375, and the 1899 date is also mentioned in a letter from W. Rössler to the India Office, 6th October 1914, IOR-L-PJ-6-1343.

11   Rössler is shown in *Thacker's* intermittently in 1903, 1906, 1910, 1912, 1914 and 1915, in all cases at 30 Creek Row, this after a non-exhaustive search of *Thacker's* over this period.

12   Many thanks to Clare Harris for this fact and reference, which was disclosed in a suit against him in the *Times of India*, September 1, 1916. Paar was a prolific publisher of court-sized cards of Darjeeling.

13   Dutta, Krishna, *Calcutta A Cultural and Literary History*, Oxford, Singal Books, 2003; p. 11.

in 1906 that "in recent years natives have more strongly than ever felt that colonialism was impossible to endure" and that they prefer "to purchase as little from English businesses and favor unfamiliar merchants."[14] I point this out here because what may have given Rössler an initial advantage in his business would later prove fateful—he was both an outsider to India, and an outsider within the British colonial apparatus that governed it.

Rössler was not one of Calcutta's major photographers. Few of his photographs seem to survive in the albums of British residents who returned home with them. Calcutta was home to great photography firms such as Bourne & Shepherd (founded 1864) and Johnston and Hoffmann (1880). One wonders if his clients were not mainly continental Europeans—for there were quite a few central European merchants, photographers, artists, archaeologists, and scholars that came out to serve as co-colonists. Many were genuinely interested in this distant civilization. Most of Rössler's postcards in fact were sent by Central Europeans (Germans, Austrians, Hungarians, Czechs and Italians). William Rössler may or may not have been related to the family of Arthur Rössler (1871–1955), the renowned Secession art critic and theorist, or Rudolf Rössler, a lithographer listed as active in Vienna in 1907.[15] He certainly was educated, as one would guess from his meticulous handwriting in later letters and the postcards he himself mailed, one to Dr. Leo Bouchal, the head of the Austrian Geographer's Society.[16] In any case, he may also have been pursuing other, less visible businesses

---

14   Schleicher elaborated was later quoted in the article as saying that "the hate against the British goes so far, that a Victoria driver did not want to take a fare further because he was smoking an English cigarette, and a shopkeeper declined another customer because he wore American boots (American because of language being taken for English)." *Papier Zeitung* No. 57 (19 July) 1906. Many thanks to Helmfried Luers, editor of *The Postcard Collector*, for this information.

15   Khan, Omar, *Paper Jewels Postcards from the Raj*, Ahmedabad, Mapin Publishing/ Alkazi Foundation for the Arts; p. 52. Rudolf Rössler is listed in the records of the Albertina, Vienna.

16   Personal communication from Ratnesh Mathur, Dec. 19, 2018, referring to a postcard sent by Rössler on October 21, 1897 from a Calcutta address (8,

in Calcutta: he sent one of his own postcards to Karl Hatta in Bohemia, Austria, in English, "A merry Xmas and a happy New Year to you" and signed it as the representative of another firm.[17]

The postcard: a European invention and its introduction in India

The concept of the postcard was invented by an Austrian in 1869, and it is no accident that Rössler had his Calcutta series printed there, most likely in Vienna's 6th district. There, lithographic presses weighing hundreds of kilos were fit into the basement rooms of five storied Hapsburg apartment buildings with large courtyards, small business at its best. Printers vied to bring out the most colorful and resonant examples of lithographic printing; sunsets were a competitive battlefield. The more colors, crayons and paper could dazzle the eye like fine pastries the better. Vienna was the cutting-edge of European postcard manufacture around 1895. In 1897, the tri-language (English, German, French) journal *The Illustrated Post-card*, the "Official Organ of the 'International Association of Collectors of Illustrated Postcards', Vienna" heralded this new illustrated mass communications medium. It focused on printing processes and examples of fine art. The Czech (Roessler's Bohemia is now part of the Czech Republic) Art Nouveau painter Alphonse Mucha designed postcards and flagship 6th district printer Philipp & Kramer's exquisitely designed works for the medium today command the highest praise and prices. "Postcard printing is one of the most beautiful branches of lithographic art," wrote Oscar Meta, a master printer in a trade journal in Vienna in 1898.[18] High technical aptitude

---

Chowringhee road). As discussed above, this was the address of Bourne & Shepherd, where he was apparently still employed as an assistant.

17   Postmarked Calcutta December 3, 1898, Author's Collection. He signs it [*Recto*] "W. Rössler Representierung [Representing] J.G.d.A. [sp?]."

18   Meta, Oscar, *Freie Künste Fachblatt für die Lithografie, Steindruckerei und Buchdruckerei [Journal of Lithography, Stone Printing and Book Printing]*, Vienna, Leipzig, No.1, 1898/1; p. 34.

was demanded. The design had to be inscribed finely with a burin on limestone, on separate twenty-five kilo blocks for each major color. The choice of dyes and chalks (Oscar Meta recommended "Bologna chalk"[19]) was critical.[20] The registration of stone vs. paper had to be perfect each time to not look even slightly mis-printed, which many early cards do, including Rössler's Calcutta cards as close examination bears witness—image titles can be a little misaligned, colors bleed beyond the outlines (see below).[21] The size of the printing "bow" or unit on many of these presses allowed for 20–24 postcard sized images to be sent through at one time. Bows were worked on for days, as paper had to dry properly before the next of a dozen or more colors was applied. The type of paper and how it absorbed inks mattered. Titles and any inscriptions on the back ("electrotype") had to be run separately.[22] Every choice was costly and consequential. Many firsts in postcard publishing were celebrated in *The Illustrated Post-Card*. These included the first artist-signed postcards of India in July 1898 by the Viennese landscape painter Josef Hoffman (1831–1904).[23] The same issue advertised a series of eighteen postcards "in finest display" of "Calcutta, Himalaya" by Hugo Bolke at 12 Government Lane, Calcutta (only one of which I have ever seen).[24] This was at least eighteen months *after* the first Rössler card was postmarked December 2, 1896 in Calcutta.

Yet it hardly came too soon: local competitors like Johnston & Hoffmann and retailer Thacker, Spink & Co. released similar lithographic

---

19   Ibid., No. 3, 1 Feb 1898; p. 33.

20   Ibid., No. 12; p. 183.

21   Rössler's *Greetings from India* cards often have the elephant grossly misaligned, which makes me think it might have been printed earlier than some of the Calcutta cards.

22   Ibid., No. 3, 1 Feb 1898; p. 33.

23   Die Illustrierte Postkarte. The Illustrated Post-Card. La Carte Postale Illustrée.Vienna, No. 7, July 1, 1898; p. 15.

24   Ibid.; p. 14. The single Bolke card known to me thus far is *Greetings from Darjeeling*, a three-panel court-sized lithograph dated March 18, 1898, Mathur Collection.

multi-view "Greetings from" Calcutta postcards by the end of 1897.[25] (Incidentally, the first cards of India published in Britain are from 1902,[26] the colonial metropolis more advanced than the motherland.) A large part of the initial regional and global market, as *The Illustrated Post-Card* articles and notes from correspondents makes clear, was driven by collectors. Many of these were women: postcard albums were usually put together by women, most cards from India and even these very early Calcutta cards by W. Rössler & Co. were sent *to* women. Female aesthetic tastes and portraits were integral to the postcard's rise.[27]

Fig. 12: "Snake Charmers", Omar Khan Collection.

---

25   Examples in the Mathur Collection (*Greetings from Calcutta*, Thacker, Spink & Co., postmarked December 1897), and Author's Collection (*Greetings from Calcutta*, Johnston & Hoffmann, postmarked Calcutta, December 2, 1898).

26   The first British-published postcards from India I have found thus far were from F. Hartmann & Co., 45 Farringdon Street, London, and were announced in *The Picture Postcard and Collector's Chronicle*, London, Dec. 1902 and advertised in the February 1903 issue. Hartmann, an indigo merchant with business in India, helped push the British postal authorities to accept the divided back postcard in 1902.

27   See Khan, *Paper Jewels, op.cit.*; p. 72.

International orchestration on many levels brought the product to market. Rössler would ship photographs from Calcutta to Vienna, the scenes in these six cards seem mainly to be from his photographs. He may or may not have worked with a design template, and/or given suggestions to the printer. In Europe proofs were often exchanged between printer and publisher before the final order was made, and it is hard to see how Rössler would not have been part of their design. Once settled, it took a month or two for cards to be shipped back for sale in retail outlets like Rössler's studio on Creek Row, just off Chowringhee road. Each print run was one or two thousand postcards, but in those early days a few hundred might comprise a reasonable order as well.

The Calcutta series: a visual approach

Let us turn to the cards and their performance of the city. All six cards feature views of Calcutta and two primary subjects or objects, people, and buildings. There are three or four major images per card aside from design and vegetal elements and identifying titles. About a quarter of each postcard, sometimes up to a third, is left blank for a message. This space sets off the rich color and design of the lithographed area. Each card has a significant image of Indian "types," which we will use to refer to them: *Indian Beauty*, *Native Ayah* [Nanny], *Nautch* [Dancing] *Girl*, *Fakir* [Holy Man], *Snake Charmers*, and *Bengaleee Babos* [Babu or Clerk]. Five cards are pedestalled with Hindu gods and goddesses. One, *Fakir*, seems to balance the old East and the new West. A single card, *Nautch Girl*, has only Indian themes on all panels. The cards are of varying quality. *Fakir* shows the most blotchiness of color compared, say, to *Snake Charmers* (one sender of *Fakir* in 1898 claimed it was "not particularly beautiful"[28]).

---

28   *Calcutta Fakir* postally used April 14, 1898, Mathur Collection. "Den 14. April 1898. Mein liebes Maronitti, hiermit haltest du die letzte der Ansichtskarten, die hier herausgekommen sind. Wenn sie auch nicht besonders schön ist, so illustrierte sie doch gut, das ganze indische Leben u. Treiben. Mit besten Grüßen an Onkel, Tante u. Dieter [sp?]. Dein Cousin, Adolf." ["April 14, 1898. My dear Maronitti, Here you have the last of the postcards that were published here even if it is not

One electrotype font is used on one card, another on three, one does not have "Made in Austria for W. Rössler, Calcutta" in the corner. The master-title "Calcutta" is lettered differently on each, and the little image titles vary in font too. While they may have been intended as a series of six—the standard for a set—the cards could have been printed at different times, even one printer changing methods along the way. The back is identical across all six cards. From what we can tell, Rössler only made one order of this set of Calcutta cards, either separately or together. The argument for separate printings is strengthened by the fact that around this time he also published single *Greetings from Darjeeling* and *Greetings from India* lithographic postcards in a similar style, with identical backs, maybe in smaller volumes than the Calcutta set.[29] These were, after all, start-up days for printers in Austria. Rössler was just emerging on his own, the medium was certainly brand new to India.

Four postcards are dominated by Western buildings, and they seem to take up the most visual space, about a quarter to a third across the cards, maybe just a bit more than the people. Postcards are an extension of architecture—if you cannot visit the place, it visits you. "Historical monuments, one can argue, live their modern lives primarily as images," writes Tapati Guha-Thakurta.[30] We should also note how sharply buildings and people are separated in these cards. Thomas R. Metcalf describes how "Indian decorative motifs," among which we can include the people and deities sprinkled throughout the cards, "one might say,

---

particularly beautiful, it does illustrate Indian life and drive. With best wishes to Uncle, Auntie and Dieter [sp?]. Your cousin Adolf."]

29   The *Greetings from India* cards (postmarks go back to Jan. 7, 1897) seem affected by a registration problem alluded to above (fn. 21). Rössler's *Greetings from Darjeeling* postcard (postmarked Calcutta 2 January 1900, Author's Collection) uses what may be an image of Sherap Gyatso, the much-photographed lama identified by Clare Harris in *Photography in Tibet*; p. 41–42. He is a bit indistinct and is holding his prayer wheel in his left hand, suggesting that if the basis was a photograph, it was reversed along the way.

30   Guha-Thakurta, Tapati, "The Compulsions of Visual Representation in Colonial India," in: Pelizzari, Maria Antonella (ed.), *Traces of India*, Montreal/New Haven, Canadian Centre for Architecture/Yale Center for British Art, 2003; p. 110.

had much in common with a classically styled architecture in India. The one announced a fascination with India, the other an assertion of control over it, but neither constructed a vision that incorporated these people and their buildings in an architecture of empire."[31] The most different card of the six and interesting for its dialectic is *Indian Beauty*. The sprawling Roman Government House that symbolized British Calcutta pours outwards to a seated woman who visually stops it cold. Beneath her feet, people are being cremated. Whether or not the composer was evoking the city's chief patron, the goddess Kali, is not known. Nicely woven atop a Grecian column on the woman's right sits another god, Ganesha, overlooking the city and also silently confronting the thrust of Government House. The contrast of Western buildings and Indian people and powers is a theme across all the cards. No Europeans are shown on any of the six cards.

"Architecture represented the authority of Britain's Raj in the colonial city from the outset," writes Metcalf. "By its very nature, indeed, the colonial city embodied an assertion of conquest. Two buildings, placed strategically at its very heart, made visible its essential character: a massive fort and an imposing Government House."[32] The many photographs in albums of Calcutta's premiere building in albums of former British residents, other postcards like a popular interior shot in Government House of a huge Grecian-columned room with chandeliers[33] make the building's iconic status for Europeans clear. "Isolated at the head of the Calcutta *maidan*," writes Metcalf, "in its own extensive compound, marked by neo-classical gates crowned by lions, without even trees to obscure the view, the Government House loomed over the city, so that all might see, and appreciate, the power of the Raj."[34] In the message area of this card, sent on November 24, 1898 from Calcutta to a Miss Jane P.

31   Metcalf, Thomas R., *An Imperial Vision Indian Architecture and Britain's Raj*, London, Faber & Faber, 1989; p. 18.
32   Ibid.; p. 8.
33   *Calcutta. Government House Throne Room* was a popular view, both in black and white and hand-tinted collotype versions published by D. Macropolo & Co.
34   Metcalf, *An Imperial Vision*; p. 14.

Barnes at the Hotel Britannique in Naples, Italy,[35] a sender who goes by
"Restless Spirit" offers choice verses in German,[36] tossing the card into
yet another dimension:

> Summer takes with it the flower's bloom
> Which allowed us such brief laughter
> A cold wind growls through forest and floors
> And rolls life's lint at our feet
> What leaves, what leaves
> Best wishes from Restless Spirit.

Most of Rössler's Calcutta cards that have survived have messages on
them. While these remain particular and at times deeply meaningful to
the people involved in a way that we cannot fathom today, they remind
us that the visual terrain of a postcard can be no less significant than the
words that are threaded through it.

Back to postcards *sans* messages. Western classical buildings dominate the horizontal space on five of the six cards. They are on top in four
of them. About thirty percent of the combined visual spaces, the largest
proportion on the six cards, consists of these modernizing structures:
besides Government House, we see the General Post Office, the Writer's
Buildings, the High Court (standing firmly against Durga and Pagoda,
taking just a bit more space), and the Great Eastern Hotel and the Telegraph Office. The latter two flank *Snake Charmers*, The two buildings
can barely be contained by their frames with the menacing, protective

---

35   In 2018 I wrote (*PaperJewels*; p. 35): "The postcard seems to have the year stamp
      of 1895 on it, but because I have found no cards clearly postmarked from 1896,
      and the fact that the earliest cards from a number of series start in 1897, I am
      inclined to think the 5 is an 8, and it was 1898." (*PaperJewels*; p. 32) That, the new
      evidence that Rössler card in the Mathur Collection is from 1896, and a closer
      look at one cancellation which could be from 1896, make dating this card very
      difficult, but the Naples 189X cancellation seems most likely to be 1898, but
      1895 cannot be ruled out.

36   [*Verso*] *Der Sommer entflieht mit ihm die Blütenpracht / Die uns so trost so wonning-
      zugelacht / Ein Kalter Wind durch Wald und Flurengrollt / Des Lebens Lenz uns vor die
      Fusserollt / Welke Blaetter, Welke Blaetter / Herzliche Grüße vom Restless Spirit.*

goddess Durga between them. Adjacent to the message space a snake charmer offers a melody to a cobra. The tension and color in *Snake Charmers* rewards looking more closely and unpacking the tiny titles. As one's eye travels along its contours and the palm fronds, noticing the pink and blue alterations in block-shadowed letters that proclaim "CALCUTTA," and the careful arrangement of people and carriages on the roads it seems as if a moving picture has been spun out of nothing. The Telegraph Office and Great Eastern Hotel were portals of communication with the homeland for colonists, the primary customer for Rössler, evoking the people and news going in and out of the city. It is hard to overestimate the importance of the telegraph to European residents. Introduced to India in 1840, the Telegraph Office was built in the 1870s. As Megan Easton Ellis writes: "A brief recital of communication timings demonstrates the irruptive powers of the telegraph ... In 1868, a telegraph sent from Calcutta to Karachi took 17 hours and 48 minutes to transmit. By 1870, the same message transmitted in a blistering speed of 4 hours and 43 minutes. In 1875, a telegraph was transmitted from London to Bombay in five minutes."[37] The acre-sized Great Eastern Hotel (1851) in the top left of *Snake Charmers* was described "one of the largest and best appointed hotels in India," whose "average stock of wines and spirits kept for the hotel's requirements is of a value of £20,000, while the assortments of preserved food dainties of every description in its storage sections represents the choicest comestibles that the world can supply."[38]

We should add that hotels were frequent subjects of early postcards, often commissioned by them to advertise their availability, a viral invite from sender to receiver, just as each of Rössler's six cards was silently prefacing "Greetings from" to "Calcutta." The crudest of the six cards, discussed earlier, is Fakir.

---

37   Robb Eaton, Megan, *Print and the Urdu Public*, New York, Oxford University Press, 2021; p. 64. Éléonore Muhidine's India collection has an analogous postcard of a modern telephone exchange.

38   Macmillan, Allister, *Seaports of India Ceylon*, London, W H & L Collingridge, 1928; p. 108.

Fig. 13: Kolkata, The "Black Hole" Memorial, symbol of
British colonial system in India.

Amazingly, although it is virtually impossible to find an example of a
publisher or photographer expressing their perspective or intentions on
a postcard, we have an example of *Fakir* which was sent by Rössler in his
own handwriting! It is one of at least four signed and sent by him, suggesting an enthusiastic proponent of his own product. On a copy of *Fakir*
sent from Calcutta to S. Gouthier, Esq. Turkenstrasse 95 [Turk's Street],
Munich, Germany, Rössler writes: "30. December 1897. When one looks
more closely at certain inhabitants of these lands, one starts to compre-
hend Darwin's theory. W Rössler."[39] Rössler's text reminds us that while
meaning could or could not be resident in a postcard, or its maker's intentions, the perceptual apparatus the viewer brought to bear was part of
the story, nudged or not by words. Rössler is connecting his set of beliefs
to the scientific theory of evolution, as racism so often is and was. Many
participants in colonial postcard exchange wore similar filters and would
have seen in the arrangement of figures and spaces their own sentiments
about Indians and superior Western culture. For them, Rössler's Indians arranged in frames in each of the postcards are strange and inferior,

---

39   Original German: "Wenn man gewisse Bewohner dieser Breiten näher betrach-
      tet, fängt man an die Darwinische Theorie zu begreifen. W. Rössler." See also:
      Khan, *Paper Jewels*; p. 42.

while the buildings are familiar and inviting, symbols of their beneficial presence. Another sender of *Fakir*, one Adolf claimed on April 14, 1898 that "it does illustrate Indian life and drive." The fakir is contrasted with the defining Hooghly Bridge cutting across the middle of the postcard, over the river that bisects Calcutta (for a very popular, more crowded single view, see Éléonore Muhidine's *The Pontoon Bridge on the Hooghly*, 1902). Once our eyes cross the bridge, a factory tower spews smoke in the distance.[40] To the right of this diagonal axis of the modern, a bathing ghat juts awkwardly against the frame of the Hooghly Bridge, described by a postcard sender as "the largest pontoon bridge in the world."[41] Built in 1874, and only meant to last 25 years, the center was "movable so as to admit of the passage of vessels up and down the river,"[42] and was only replaced in the 1940s. Each of these postcards is negotiation between modern European and ancient—or, to Rössler and much of his community, primitive—Indian forms and practice.

Fig. 14: Kolkata, The old pontoon bridge (1874).

40   Ibid.; p. 43.

41   *CALCUTTA The Hooghly Bridge*, G. Valsecchi & Co., Calcutta, postally used May 7, 1907 sent to Mrs. W.J. Hamlin in New Jersey, USA, Mathur Collection.

42   *A Handbook for Travellers in India Burma and Ceylon*, London, John Murray, 1938; p. 106.

Postcards and architectural views in the colonial context

Rössler's cards were part of a shared visual vocabulary. Another very early popular card of the city, *Calcutta*, a single-image lithograph by Budapest-based Cosmos-Publishing also emphasized the modern part of the city, neo-classical buildings with inset columns and billowing red-and-white Parisian-style blinds. Thacker, Spink & Co. offered its own multi-view, court-sized black and white halftones as early as 1898, featuring harbour scenes where European ships dominated.[43] They also published a three-panelled *Hindoo Temple, Jain Temple Manicktola* with a *Hindoo Fakir* in the same left pole position as in Rössler's *Fakir* postcard. D. Macropolo & Co., the Raj's largest tobacco retailer, offered multi-view lithographic post-cards by 1900, including a *Greetings from India* that was strikingly similar to Rössler's in lettering and colors, three identical images arranged slightly differently.[44] Johnston & Hoffman, Rössler's former employer, would also opt for the multi-view lithograph *Greetings from Calcutta*, with two panels intertwined among palm fronds and curling around the Telegraph Office and a tram rolling into the distance while native boats crowd on the riverbank between scores of fuzzy black bodies like those in the right pane of Rössler's *Fakir*. Still, prejudice wrapped in beauty need not be the only part of the story in these cards.

Bengali Babos [Babu] includes two more buildings key to representing the Raj. The Post Office was another temple to communication, opened

---

43   Court-sized collotype versions of *Shipping on the* Hooghly, Thacker, Spink & Co., Calcutta, c. 1898 and 1900 are good examples. An earlier version (1898?) has elaborate palms around ship sails spilling out of the vignette image covering about a third of the court-sized card. A little later (1900?) the same space was occupied by the sailboats in a rectangular frame without the design fussiness and a printed title in the front, illustrating how quickly styles and maybe costs changed in the postcard market.

44   An example of the Macropolo version was postally used September 10, 1899, Author's Collection. This was said to be printed in Italy, which suggests that design elements could belong to the publisher or be sent from one printer to the other, or perhaps most likely held in some form by the publisher, e.g. Rössler.

in 1865, the largest in India, said to have been constructed on the "Black Hole" where many Europeans died during an Indian uprising.

Fig. 15: Bengali Babos, Collection Omar Khan.

The Writer's Buildings is where all the men who came out to India to make their fortunes in the East India Company began their work (they "wrote" an exam for the privilege) and by now housed the Bengal state government. The horizontal spread—"expressing the expanding power of the British Raj as it grew to encompass all of India," in Metcalf's words[45]—is the cleanest looking. So as is the deft splicing together two corners of the maidan into one visual line with a palm tree. The neatly clad babu is welcoming you to the city, with an umbrella that shields and separates him from the buildings. He conveys a certain authority over his space including the long white writing surface spread in front of him.[46] The Palladian columns of the Post Office in the panel above extend his halo. He is not the same type as the fakir, perhaps a step up the species ladder, Herr Rössler? It is hard to tell of course. "Properly a

45   Metcalf, *An Imperial Vision*; p. 12.
46   The Indian painter M.V. Dhurandhar's signed postcard *Bengalee Babu*, Unknown Publisher, Bombay, c. 1904 is a more complex portrait of this oft-maligned type. See Khan, *Paper Jewels*; p. 37.

term of respect attached to a name, like *Master* or Mr., and formerly in some parts of Hindustan applied to certain persons of distinction," went Hobson-Jobson, the bible of Raj terminology (1903) when explaining that babu, "in Bengal and elsewhere, among Anglo-Indians, it is often used with a slight savour of disparagement, as characterizing a superficially cultivated, but too often effeminate, Bengali."[47]

Maybe. The babu also represented a certain balance between the European and the Indian. The Maharashtrian postcard artist M.V. Dhurandhar had a much more sympathetic *Bengalee Babu* with the umbrella on his side in dhoti and waist jacket. In short, people read the babu many ways, and Rössler's card lets you do that. The owner of the card seems to appreciate his, and simply marked it with initials in the bottom right corner, something like *G.E.D. 1/7 97*, in careful (but careless!) pen strokes next to "W. Rössler Calcutta." While postcards can and do engage people's prejudices and assumptions, they can also deflect and recast them, as the Babu might to those who have the receptivity to see him in other ways. The very putting of things, people and place into play is what made these early lithographic cards appealing. Not to say that postcards do not embody a maker's—photographer's, designer's, lithographer's—biases, which may be unambiguous to them and contradictory, but that those intentions can be moderated, intensified, contradicted by their juxtaposition in the early lithographic multi-view postcard. Whether or not Rössler's six Calcutta lithographs were successful commercially is hard to tell. They are postmarked well into the early 1900s. Rössler put out black and white single image court-sized collotypes around the time he opened his store in 1899, including of images that he had used in the lithographic cards like *CALCUTTA. Nautch Girl*.[48]

One of Rössler's early collotypes, *Government House—Calcutta*, showed the building's other side and was made likely from a photo-

---

47   Yule, Henry; Burnell, A.C., *Hobson-Jobson*, London, John Murray, 1903; p. 44. The definition of Babu continues: "And from the extensive employment of the class, to which the term was applied as a title, in the capacity of clerks in English offices, the word has come often to signify 'a native clerk who writes English.'"

48   See: Khan, *Paper Jewels*; p. 40.

graph that was also used by Thacker, Spink & Co. in a hand-tinted colour version,[49] suggesting that Rössler licensed some of his images. From this angle, the building seems to spread its wings.

Fig. 16: Government House—Calcutta, Rössler, Omar Khan Collection.

CALCUTTA.   GOVERNMENT HOUSE.

Note the telephone wires not airbrushed out by either publisher. Barely twenty years old, they were fresh as daisies to Calcutta's residents. Rössler's collotypes are rich in tone, with compelling portraits like *Bengali Girl* and *Bengal Village Scene*.[50] Many of the collotypes like *Government House—Calcutta* were of course of buildings already discussed, some in multiple views. This "colonial adaptation of the Palladian style" as Lord Curzon described it, was still strong and desirable in Curzon's opinion for the Victoria Memorial he was about to help design, more than a century after Government House, but needed adjustments for its "severity," an index perhaps of what (little) had changed.[51] Even with

---

49   *Government House—CALCUTTA.*, coloured collotype, Thacker, Spink & Co., Calcutta, c. 1902, p.u. Lahore 25.8.04, Author's Collection.

50   *Bengali Girl*, W. Rössler, court-sized collotype, sent to a Mrs. Agnes Rössler in Bohemia, Austria, and signed from "W & L," postmarked Calcutta Dec. 13, 1908 [?], Author's Collection. For *Bengal Village Scene*, W. Rössler, court-sized collotype, see Khan, *Paper Jewels*; p. 36.

51   Metcalf, *An Imperial Vision*; p. 235.

collotype postcards ("Made in Austria"), commercial success seems to have been elusive for Rössler. Their quality was high, but it is hard to find examples today, suggesting that the batches were small. He did make it into regular-sized collotype postcards around 1901–02, but these too are uncommon compared to those of competitors previously cited, all of whom published postcards in much larger volumes in the first years after 1900.

Rössler's impossible return to India

By 1905, Rössler seems to have abandoned the postcard business altogether. The first but minor player, just like lithographic cards were to collotypes and all that followed. Unforeseen for him, William Rössler's adventures were only beginning. Whatever he might have thought or intended to illustrate with his postcards about East and West, the colonial coalition was to fracture, severely jolting his own relationship to the city. On April 17, 1913 Louisa Rössler died of "vascular disease of the heart and edema of the lungs."[52] In November that year he would marry again the widow Margaret S. ("Carrie") Greiff from a Bengal civil family of modest means and of German origin. Her former husband was a stationmaster, her brother a pensioner in England.[53] Five months later, the newly-weds appear in the *Times of India* on the "list of passengers proceeding to Trieste and Venice via intermediate ports, per Austrian Lloyd's steamer Gablonz on the 1st May from the Alexandra Dock No.

---

52   Burials at the Military Cemetery of Fort William Bengal Archdiocese of Calcutta entry for April 13, 1913; p. 204, N-1-389, seen on FindmyPast.com, February 2023.

53   See letter dated 6 October 1914 from J.C. Greiff to the India Office, IOR-L-PJ-6-1343. Margaret S. gave birth to a daughter, Margaret Beryl, on Dec. 4, 1893 in Khagole, Bengal, where her husband, Julius A. S. Greiff, is described in the record as a Stationmaster, Parish register transcripts from the Presidency of Bengal, N-1-286. In another record, her father, Julius Greiff is described as a "Guard, E.I.R. [East Indian Railways]," Birth record for Lionel Walter Kirkpatrick, May 17, 1885 in: Asanol Bengal, Parish Record Transcripts from Bengal, Record N-1-202 both seen on FindmyPast.com February 2023.

4 [Bombay]. The medical inspection of the saloon passengers with take place at the Alexandra Dock Shed No. 4 on the same day at 1–30 a.m. Deck passengers and Native servants must be present at the port *Health Disinfecting Station, Frere Road*, near Prince's Dock, with all their luggage and kit, at 9 a.m. sharp."[54] Three months later, in August 1914, World War I broke out. Two months later this letter was received by the Chief Secretary to the Govt. of India, Bengal, and then apparently copied to the Secretary to the Govt. of India, Home Department, Delhi:

"To the India Office.

Sir,

The undersigned, an Austrian Subject of over 50 years of age, who has been living in Calcutta since 1898 and has a photographic business there since 1899 left Calcutta at the end of April last year with his wife to pay a visit to his people in Bohemia.

Now he finds himself unable to return to India and therefore addresses the India Office if they could furnish him with the necessary papers for a safe return...

A line in reply at an early date will much oblige.

Yours etc.

W. Rössler

c/o Mrs. Lydia Sebald, Internazional Traktsgesellschaft, 23 Nonnenweg, Basel, Switzerland."[55]

His request was not granted. Later that month he wrote again to the Home Department in Delhi:

"He is anxious to become a British subject, because all his interests are in India. It may be mentioned here that he is over 50 years of age. His wife was born in India and has passed all her life there. Four of her children 2 sons and 2 daughters are in India and the younger of the latter is

---

54 *The Times of India*, Bombay, April 29, 1914; p. 10.
55 Letter to the India Office from W. Rössler, dated October 6, 1914, IOR-L-PJ-6-1343.

depending on him for support. The undersigned has tried every possible means for obtaining the necessary papers for a safe return to India but has failed up to now. Having been advised by the British Consul in Geneva to apply to India for a permit to return he applied, through lack of information, to the Foreign Office. Please address. W. Rössler."[56]

The second letter was filled with a list of references including "the official Trustee of Bengal, whose tenant he has been for over 17 years" [this would put Rössler's going into business in 1897, within a year of the first postcards] and other senior civil officials. On December 11th, a letter in Rössler's neat handwriting, each word slowly pressed into paper, was sent to the Secretary of State for India in London: "The undersigned is in great distress and begs the India Office to grant him a conditional permit for a return to India ... his distress increases with each single day of delay, he most earnestly prays the India Office for help, by granting him such a permit ..."[57] Six days later he is again referred to the authorities in India by an Assistant Secretary. The British government could not see him as an ally, even after so many years supporting the colonial enterprise and marrying a British woman. Government House now condemned him.

The prejudice against Indians that had in part driven the British community in Calcutta was quickly directed against Germans and Austrians. In the crisis leading up to the break out of war, the a European Association of Calcutta's request called "attention to the strong public feeling that exists in India in favour of taking drastic steps for the immediate internment of all German and Austrian aliens who are now residing at large in that country;" it was discussed in the House of Commons.[58] Indeed, originally Austrian photographers like Thomas Paar and German

---

56   Letter to the Secretary to the Government of India, Home Dept. Delhi from W. Rössler, received Dec. 18, 1914. The original letter was received by the Chief Secretary to the Government of Bengal on October 22, 1914. IOR-L-PJ-6-1343.

57   Letter to the Secretary of State for India from W. Rössler, December 11, 1914, to the India Office IOR-L-PJ-6-1343.

58   Copy Questions discussed in the House of Commons on Thursday, 16 September 1915 referring to two letters from June 12 and August 15, 1915 from the European Association of Calcutta IOR-L-PJ-6-1400 3602.

ones would see their businesses destroyed.[59] Many were sent to camps like Ahmednagar, admittedly a rather open camp where some German-speaking lithographers could pass the time making amateur postcards showing themselves suffering in the sun and send them to relatives in Germany.[60] The treatment of Rössler's many petitions to the India Office over the years was not exceptional: American citizens of Swiss origin were restricted in travel,[61] German wives of inmates at Ahmednagar were sent back home despite protesting medical conditions,[62] neutral citizens like those from Switzerland who were suspected of pro-German sympathies were prevented from returning to employment in Bombay,[63] and more.[64]

Longstanding relationships that had been formed among colonists were dissolved, whether on the basis of their citizenship, national origin, or stated or private opinions. Anyone had the privilege of becoming

59   Thomas Paar's photography business was listed under the heading "Winding Up Hostile Firms," August 5, 1916 in *The Times of India*, Simla, Aug. 7, 1907, as was the business of Fritz Capp, photographer of Calcutta and Dacca.

60   *Fröhliche Weihnacht*, for example, is a crude, hand-made lithographic card showing a European seating in the sun and sent from "H. Pome, "Prisoners of war Camp Ahmednagar 19.11.19" to Fräulein M. Pome in Austria, Author's Collection. This camp held over 1,100 prisoners by August 1915, per Communique from the Home Dept. August 13, 1915, IOR-L-PJ-6-1399 (3517).

61   See the case of an American citizen, O. Nussman, whose travel was restricted leading to protests by the American authorities in 1915, IOR-L-PJ-6-1399 (3517).

62   See the case of Frau Rosenthal, "German lady in India," wife of an inmate at Ahmednagar, and mother of a young child who apparently was sent back to Germany in 1916 despite a request from the American government to treat her case with sympathy, IOR-PJ-6-1427 (573).

63   See the case of the exclusion of Mr. Oscar Bruderer "on account of strong pro-German sympathies," as communicated by the India Office to the Foreign Office on October 26, 1915, IOR-L-PJ-6-1403 (4024–4028).

64   See for example the voluminous file and discussion of this subject as it applied to citizens of the US, Sweden, Norway, Denmark and Switzerland undergoing special scrutiny, IOR-L-PJ-6-1411 (4487) and the examination of letters and other material to solicit their true sympathies, IOR-L-PJ-6-1444 (2503).

an alien. On June 1st, 1915 *The Times of India* carried this story under the headline *Calcutta German Killed*:

> "At least one citizen of Calcutta, who has been killed on the German side fighting against his will, too, was Mr. W. Rössler, a photographer... When the war broke out he was swept, despite his protestations of ill-health and age (he was over 50), into the army and was killed at Neuve Chapelle [France] after being at the front only two days. A pathetic letter from his death and her arrival in London whither she has been sent by the German Government."[65]

Only nothing of the sort happened. His wife, Carrie Rössler was actually with him in Basel, Switzerland, appealing to the Under Secretary of State for India:

> "For in our distress we are at a loss what to do, unless we appeal to your goodness... We are informed that during the continuance of the war a permit cannot be granted us to return to India. Under these circumstance we are simply left to face misery, ruin & starvation, for all the time we are away from our home in Calcutta, we have no sort of income, & our home & property may all be destroyed. We have had only one letter from our children in India..."[66]

Like Rössler's, her neat script suggests someone of education and literacy. Around the time Rössler was reported killed, her brother was writing similar pleading letters, recounting her four children in Calcutta, all British subjects, three young, one "working as an engineer on a government steamer."[67] The bureaucracy remained unmoved. In July 1918, "after finally turning his back on his native land (3rd January 1916) and living over one year and a half in Switzerland," and receiving "a formal discharge from Austrian citizenship," from Zurich he "most earnestly begs

---

65   *The Times of India*, Bombay June 1, 1915; p. 8.

66   Letter to the Under Secretary of State for India, Public Department, London, from Carrie Rössler, December 28, 1914, IOR-L-PJ-6-1343.

67   Letter to the Under Secretary of State for India, India Office, London from J. C. Greiff, April 17, 1915. IOR-L-PJ-6-1343.

that the plea of a perishing victim of circumstance may be acceded to and has the honour to be Sir Most Respectfully Yours W. Rössler."[68] But this is impossible, for now it has come out that he may have served with the German army, another flag for Government who also know about the (false) report that he was killed. It is hard to know how and why the report of his demise may have been manufactured, but it is possible that there is a grain of truth in it, that he was conscripted to the front –though why the German front in France and not the Austrian in the Balkans? Maybe he was in Germany, trying to flee the Austrian authorities, and staged his death by newspaper to flee to Switzerland, a neutral country from where petitions, however, started coming in October 1914. We likely will never know. Finally, when the war was over, Lord Curzon, who served as Viceroy in Calcutta (1899–1905) during Rössler's time interceded on his behalf.

In August 1919 the official in charge cautions Curzon that:

"Mr. Rössler does not always appear to have been strictly accurate in the statements which he has made relative to his movements since the beginning of the war: thus he informed the Passport Office here that he had not been to Germany since 1914 when he and his wife were travelling in German and Austria from 1914 up to and including 1916. In 1914 the Indian Government refused him permission to return to India on the ground of his being an enemy alien."[69]

The sticking point, and opportunity as outlined by Government now was that he had to get the new Czecho-Slovak authorities ruling Bohemia to acknowledge him as their citizen before he would be granted the permit to go back. He was now the subject of a new nation. The paper trail in a voluminous file goes cold later in the month, but Rössler seems to have made his way back to Calcutta soon thereafter. Rössler spent another decade in the city. He is listed in *Thacker's 1925* with a store at 56

---

68   Letter to the Secretary of State for India, London from W. Rössler, July 1, 1918, IOR-L-PJ-6-1343.

69   Letter to Earl Curzon of Kedleston from Horace Rumbold, August 23, 1919, IOR-L-PJ-6-1343.

Bentnick Street, though not as "Photographer." He died on November 3, 1929 and was buried with Seventh Day Adventist rites in the Military Cemetery, Calcutta, perhaps a final ignominy to his body. Like postcards, human beings wove their flags above a network of impermanent connections and shifting allegiances.

References

Anonymous, *A Handbook for Travellers in India Burma and Ceylon*, London, John Murray, 1938.

Anonymous, *Die Illustrierte Postkarte/The Illustrated Post-Card/La Carte Postale Illustrée*, Vienna, Austria, 1898–1900.

Anonymous, *Freie Künste Fachblatt für die Lithographie, Steindruckerei und Buchdruckerei [Journal of Lithography, Stone Printing and Book Printing]*, Vienna and Leipzig, 1898.

Anonymous, *Thacker's Indian Directory*, Kolkata, Thacker, Spink & Co., 1890–1935.

Anonymous, *The Picture Postcard and Collector's Chronicle*, London, 1901–04.

Alloula, Malek, *The Colonial Harem, Minneapolis*, University of Minnesota Press, 1986.

Dutta, Krishna, *Calcutta A Cultural and Literary History*, Oxford, Signal Books, 2003.

Guha-Thakurta, Tapati, "The Compulsions of Visual Representation in Colonial India," in: Pelizzari, Maria Antonella (ed.), *Traces of India*, Montreal/New Haven, Canadian Centre for Architecture/Yale Center for British Art, 2003.

The Times of India, Bombay, 1899–1921.

Harris, Clare, *Photography in Tibet*, London, Reaktion Books, 2016.

India Office Record, London, British Library, IOR-L-PJ-6-1343, IOR-L-PJ-6-1399, IOR-L-PJ-6-1403, IOR-L-PJ-6-1411, IOR-PJ-6-1427, IOR-L-PJ-6-1444, IOR-L-PJ-6-1400 3602.

Khan, Omar, *Paper Jewels Postcards from the Raj*, Ahmedabad/Delhi, Mapin/ The Alkazi Collection of Photography, 2018.

Macmillan, Allister, *Seaports of India Ceylon*, London, W. H. & L. Collingridge, 1928.

Mathur, Sangeetha; Mathur, Ratnesh, *Picturesque India, A Journey in Early Picture Postcards (1896–1947)*, Delhi, Nyogi Books, 2018.

Metcalf R., Thomas, *An Imperial Vision Indian Architecture and Britain's Raj*, London, Faber & Faber, 1989.

Neumayer, Erwin; Neumayer, Christine, *Raja Ravi Varma, Portrait of an Artist: The Diary of C. Raja Raja Varma*, Delhi, Oxford University Press, 2005.

Pinney, Christopher, *The Coming of Photography in India*, London, British Library, 2008.

Woody, Howard, "International Postcards Their History, Production and Distribution (Circa 1895–1915)," in: Geary, Christraud M.; Webb, Virgina-Lee (eds.), *Delivering Views Distant Cultures in Early Postcards*, Smithsonian Institution Press, Washington/London, 1998.

Greetings from Bombay! Pictures of Colonial Complexity

Preeti Chopra

Fig. 17: Mumbai. Bombay Bay around 1900. In the 1920s, the British colonial administration carried out new works to drain the sea and expand the city.

Say you get a post card.[1] You see a place far away, mostly beautiful, or at least interesting. You know the sender, why otherwise would they know your address or anyway send it to you? You can ask yourself: what's the message? Does the sender want your company? Is he or she lonely

---

1   I would like to acknowledge gratefully the support for this research was provided by the American Academy of Rome, the University of Wisconsin-Madison, Office of the Vice Chancellor for Research and Graduate Education with funding from the Wisconsin Alumni Research Foundation.

out there? Or just wants to make you envious? "Hey, I am here, you are not. I know you can't but would like to. Wouldn't you...?" A message from a lucky and free acquaintance from a paradisical Erehwon.[2] Turn the name of this place the other way around, and you read "Nowhere." That's not a place to be. Then you forget that and look at the image side of your newly received postcard. There! That's a place on earth. Greetings from Bombay! Welcome to the historical complexity of colonialism. Postcards give a glimpse of a place by isolating a building, a view, individuals, from the larger context. They want to spark something in you, create something new or revive something old, like nostalgia.

For this essay, I look at a selection of postcards of colonial Bombay from Éléonore Muhidine's collection of Bombay postcards. They are not sent to me. I know the city and will surely go there again when I need to. I look at them in another way. Historically. I explore the palimpsests that make up many of these sites to excavate Bombay's past. One of the definitions for palimpsest is "a manuscript in which a later writing is written over an effaced earlier one."[3] Taking this approach, postcards are released from the confines of their frame to allow for a nuanced and layered understanding of Bombay's architecture in the context of its urban setting.

The Bombay Fort and its urban design

The Fort was the nucleus of British colonial settlement and the foundation of the town and city of Bombay. The cotton boom of the 1860s encouraged the colonial government, under the leadership of Governor Sir

---

2   *Erewhon: or, Over the Range* (New York, Modern Library, 1872) is a novel by English writer Samuel Butler, first published anonymously in 1872, is in an invented country discovered and surveyed by the protagonist. At first Erewhon appears to be Utopia. The book is a satire on Victorian society.

3   *Oxford English Dictionary* (OED), second edition (1989). See https://www.oed.com/oed2/00169695. (02.02.2023).

Bartle Frere (1862–67), to finally throw down the ramparts surrounding the city in 1864, no longer necessary for military purposes.

This opened the plain, transforming the city by creating a vast new public arena for government offices and public institutions. Urban projects transformed the Fort area leading to the establishment of a north-south and east-west axes. These axes were accentuated in the subsequent decades with the construction of public buildings. The east-west axis started on the east from the Town Hall, went through the garden at Elphinstone Circle to join Church Gate Street that was adjacent to public buildings on the western rim, ending most notably with the B.B. & C.I. Railways Offices Station (1894–96)[4] and Churchgate Station, and terminated with an expansive view across Back Bay. The north-south axis culminated at the northern end with the great Victoria Terminus (1878–1887) and the Gateway of India (1927) at Apollo Bunder. These two axes intersected at what is commonly referred as Flora Fountain.[5] In *Maclean's Guide* of 1889, Rampart Row, which traces of the line of the old fortification between Apollo and Church Gates and the western boundary of South Fort, curves northwards to "the 'Grande Place' formed at this point," where "is the Frere Fountain, a very beautiful work of art."[6] Inaugurated in 1869, the fountain was first named after Bombay Governor Sir Bartle Frere, a central figure in the reshaping of Bombay.

Designed by R. Norman Shaw, the British sculptor James Forsythe worked on imported Portland stone to sculpt the fountain. The sculptures include four mythological figures as well "Flora," the Roman goddess, whose figure crowns the fountain. The fountain is located at or near the site of what was Church Gate, one of the gates into the Fort. Church

---

4   Now the Western Railway Headquarters.

5   Mehrotra, Rahul, "Bazaars in Victorian Arcades: Conserving Bombay's Historic Core," in: Dandekar C., Hemalata (ed.), *City Space + Globalization: An International Perspective*, Chicago, University of Michigan, 1998; p.46-53.

6   Maclean Mackenzie, James, *Guide to Bombay: Historical, Statistical, and Descriptive* (henceforth, *Guide to Bombay*). Fourteenth Edition, Bombay, Bombay Gazette Steam Press, 1889; p. 217. "Bazaars in Victorian Arcades" puts the date for Flora Fountain as 1887, while newspaper articles date the inauguration of the fountain to 1869. The latter is likely correct.

Gate Street owes its name to St. Thomas Church, now Cathedral since around 1838. Certainly by 1910, the fountain was referred to as the "Floral Fountain" as it is in the postcard. In the image we can see that the fountain was encircled by a grass plot and palm trees. By 1908, these were removed so that "pedestrians and horse-traffic between the tram lines and kerb of the fountain" could be accommodated.

Fig. 18: Mumbai, Esplanade Road and Floral Fountain.

In the background to the left, the tree-lined Esplanade Road leads northward. At the junction of Churchgate and Esplanade Roads stands the General Post Office, north of which is the Government Telegraph Office. Beyond these buildings stood the Queen's Statue, which is not visible. The General Post Office (1869–72) was designed by J. Trubshawe and W. Paris, both Architects to Government. W. Paris was also the architect for the Telegraph Office (1871–74), which was later expanded. These buildings have been praised for their use of the "Venetian-Gothic" style-building plans, proportions, the quality of the rich ornamentation on the front façade of the Post Office.[7] The image shows the twin towers, sharply

---

7   Maclean, *Guide to Bombay*, op.cit.; p.212-14.

sloping roofs, an arcade on the lower floor (the two-storey porch at the entrance is partially veiled by trees).

Although native contributions are mentioned in colonial-era records and guidebooks in passing, they are intrinsic to the construction of these buildings. Muncherjee Cowasjee Murzban, a native engineer from the Parsi community, was the Assistant Engineer in charge of both these buildings. His biography records an incident related to construction of the General Post Office, used since 1914 as an adjunct to the General Telegraph Office. According to this account, the construction of this building was based on designs sent out from England by an English architect. The building was designed in such a way that the entire weight of the two upper floors was to fall on the sub-structure of the ground floor comprised of columns and arches.

The Post Office building: a colonial landmark

As the building construction commenced, Murzban alerted his superior officer of the inherent weakness of the under-structure. When work on the super-structure of the two upper floors was almost complete and roofing had begun, the inadequacy of the stone columns became clear one had a complete vertical crack. Realizing that a structural collapse would tarnish the reputation of the Public Works Department (PWD), Murzban took matters in his own hands and immediately replaced the cracked column with a new one. Not long after it had been replaced, several other columns were found to be fractured under the excessive weight of the superstructure. People in Bombay began to talk about how the Post Office Building was collapsing, which reached the attention of the governor of Bombay, Sir Seymour Vesey FitzGerald. It was decided that the eight columns beneath the two upper floors should be replaced and Murzban was put in charge. It was a risky enterprise and several Indian and European engineers, the Chief Engineer and the Executive Engineer stopped by to see how this was being handled. Murzban's successful resolution of this structural crisis resulted in his promotion.[8] Even as Murzban portrayed himself as loyal to the colonial government, it appears that the tutelage of the British was no longer necessary, for both native and European engineers learned from his handling of the situation.

Fig. 19: Mumbai, Crawford Market.

From Floral to Flora Fountain

Floral Fountain was not meant for this location but was planned for the centre of Victoria Gardens at Byculla by the Agri-horticultural Society that raised funds for the purpose. After the financial crash of 1865,

---

8   Murzban, M. M., *Leaves from the Life of Khan Bahadur Muncherji Cowasji Murzban, C. I. E.: with an Introduction containing a life-sketch of Fardunji Murbanji*, Bombay, Furdoonji Byramji Marzban, 1915, p. 47–49. Murzban's son does not give a date for the building nor the name of the English architect. The General Post Office, opened on 1 December 1872, was based on designs by J. Trubshawe and W. Paris, architects to the government. Murzban was appointed as assistant to Trubshawe in 1863. See: Furneaux, J. H., *Glimpses of India: A Grand Photographic History of The Land of Antiquity, the vast Empire of the East*, Bombay, C. B. Burrows, 1895; p. 214.

the Society found itself short of funds. Arthur Crawford, president of the Society and member of the Esplanade Fee Fund Committee, came to a solution for the latter committee to pay the remaining costs and establish the fountain at this site.[9] Opposite the fountain was the newly constructed and "conspicuous Cathedral High School," which had a "medieval feeling" but was constructed in the "Modern Gothic Style" by J. Adams. Erected at the junction of the Esplanade main road and Hornby Row (later, Road), it was carefully designed as a pentagon with two rectangular wings that fronted and were parallel to the roads.[10] Instead of the High School, in the image you see the Oriental Buildings, about which more later.

Fig. 20: Mumbai, Hornby Road in the 1940s.

Merging with Rampart Row at Flora fountain, Hornby Row/Road curves northwards towards the right, as the western edge of north Fort, and a reminder of the ramparts. In 1898, design guidelines established that each building here had to have an arcade. At an urban scale, this arcade helped to unify the streetscape and give coherence to individual buildings constructed by different architects, in various architectural styles. Emphasizing the importance of this urban design intervention in

9   Maclean, *op.cit.*; p.217.
10   Ibid.; p.218.

strengthening the north-south axis, architect and conservationist Rahul Mehrotra argued that "This development along Hornby Road connected the crescent of public buildings south of Flora Fountain (including Elphinstone College, Sasson [sic] Library, the University and Watsons [sic] Hotel), unifying disparate elements in the composition of the newly designed city core."[11]

Hornby Road takes us to perhaps the finest Victorian Gothic Revival building in India, the Great Indian Peninsular Railway Victoria Terminus and Administrative Offices (1878–87), commonly known as Victoria Terminus or VT (1878–1887), which is to the right. In England, John Ruskin and others actively supported Gothic architecture, extolling its virtue as an artifact of craftsmanship rather than machine production. Ruskin and other critics of the industrial era romanticized medieval architecture as representing an era that was more honest and truthful than their own. By reviving medieval architecture, they hoped that society might recapture its dignity. Ian Baucom has argued that in the years following the Revolt of 1857–8 in India, Frere and other government officials elected to spend large amounts of money on building projects in Bombay. They believed in Ruskin's view that "the identity of the empire's subjects was to a significant degree a product of the objects and structures which they beheld and inhabited. Ruskin had spent years informing England that there was a direct relationship between the arrangements of space and the contours of the personality."[12] If Indo-Saracenic architecture aimed to remake the British as indigenous rulers, Bombay's Victorian Gothic sought, in a sense, to shape a collective personality so that the *English* might remain English, while Indians could be remade as Englishmen.

11   Mehrotra, Rahul, "Bazaars in Victorian Arcades," *op.cit.*; p.47.

12   Baucom, Ian, *Out of Place: Englishness, Empire, and the Locations of Identity*, Princeton, Princeton University Press, 1999; p.79.

Fig. 21: Mumbai, Victoria Terminus (1888), today
Chhatrapati Shivaji Terminus (CST) in the 1970s.

Buildings in which the Gothic Revival style was combined with Indic
details were confusing for the British, as they simultaneously helped
project a sense of Englishness while producing a clear degree of hybridity, thus revealing the colonial state's "capacity to collect and exhibit
alterity."[13] There are many buildings of this type in British Bombay, such
as the Law Courts (1871–9), or the Municipal Buildings (1888–93), but
among the most conspicuous is the magnificent Victoria Terminus. It
is designed by Frederick Williams Stevens and based on G.G. Scott's
Grand Midland Hotel at St Pancras Station in London (1868–77). It con-
tains Indic details that came from the hands of students and craftsmen
associated with the Bombay School of Art, under the supervision of John
Griffiths. The administrative buildings formed three sides of a square,
enclosing a garden, whose entrance gate was guarded by a huge lion
and tiger carved in stone. A triumphant figure of Progress crowned the
building's impressive dome, a life-size statue of Queen-Empress Victoria stood in front of the main façade. Commenting on the dome, Davies
notes that "Unlike St Pancras, VT is symmetrical and is surmounted by a
colossal masonry dome, ostensibly 'the first applied to a Gothic building

---

13   Ibid.; p. 85.

on scientific principles,' and this claim is probably true."[14] Glowing in his praise of Victoria Terminus, Davies correctly points out that if there was one critique to be made it would be "in the ratio of its length to its height."

Victorian Gothic architecture is associated with verticality, whereas the large foreground and almost interminable side elevation of the train shed bordering the road emphasize its horizontality, as can be seen in this view.[15] The Victoria Terminus is enmeshed in other popular histories that shape its meaning. In the second half of the nineteenth century, Bombay emerged as a major center for Islam, both in the context of its continental hinterland and as the central hub of a West Indian Ocean world. Nile Green has uncovered stories that reveal the commonly held belief that this industrial city was governed by hidden supernatural forces. One was of the shrine of a Muslim saint, Sayyid Bismillah Shah Baba, that was built into the very structure of the Victoria Terminus. Bismillah Shah was a migrant and, similar to other migrant shrines, his "unknown grave... was 'rediscovered' in miraculous circumstances." The story, according to oral tradition, suggests that when the railway was being laid the tracks in this part of the station would surprisingly disappear or break overnight. Finally, British surveyors and workmen found out that a Muslim holy man lay buried there. The railway company paid for the construction of the domed mausoleum that covers Bismillah Shah's grave, undoubtedly, to ensure that the construction of the Terminus proceeded smoothly. This then became a site of pilgrimage for travelers who made a stop here before embarking on their journey.[16] For some, it is likely that the saint's tomb was more important than Victoria as Queen-Empress, identifying the building with the saint's protection instead.

---

14   Davies, Philip, *Splendours of The Raj: British Architecture in India 1660-1947*, Harmondsworth, Penguin Books, 1985; p.173.

15   *Ibid.*; p.175.

16   Green, Nile, *Bombay Islam: The Religious Economy of the West Indian Ocean, 1840–1915*, Cambridge, Cambridge University Press, 2011; p. 63–64.

Opposite the Victoria Terminus one can see the Municipal Buildings, which stands at the junction of two prominent roads. In an editorial in 1888, the *Builder* noted that there were two opposing theories of how Anglo-Indian, or in other words, architecture as practiced by the English in India should take. One theory advocated "adopting or assimilating native styles" and was illustrated by the prize-winning design by the architect R.F. Chisholm for the proposed Municipal Offices Buildings in Bombay. Even though the design won first place it had been abandoned for reasons unknown. The second theory of Anglo-Indian architecture was to transpose European forms to India, with minor changes and the example given in the *Builder* was of Stevens's recently built Victoria Terminus.[17] Chisholm's Indo-Saracenic design for the Municipal Buildings was never built. Stevens, rather than Chisholm got the commission to design and build the Municipal Buildings (1888–93) whose gable is crowned by a winged figure that confidently symbolizes the city as "Urbs Prima in Indis." In this and increasingly in the Church Gate Terminus (1894–96) designed for the Bombay, Baroda and Central Indian Railway, Stevens tried to marry the Venetian Gothic with the Indo-Saracenic, the latter effect created mainly through the shape of the domes and domelets. However, the plan and design of Churchgate terminus is substantially like the Victoria Terminus. At this time, Stevens also undertook the refashioning of what was the Cathedral School into the Oriental Buildings at Flora Fountain. In common with Church Gate Terminus, it also employs "grey facings with bands of white stone dressings." Of the Oriental Buildings, Davies goes on to say, "It is an evocative affair with a spiky silhouette of spirelets, turrets and gables looking like a setting from some tropical *Gotterdämmerung*... it is an excellent climax in the townscape".[18]

Apart from Sir Bartle Frere's active encouragement of the use of the Gothic Revival style in Bombay in the 1860s, Stamp points to two reasons for its success in Bombay. First, one could find good stone of different colors for construction, allowing for the solid construction desired by

---

17   "Anglo-Indian Architecture", *Builder*, 1888/55; p.313.
18   Davies, *op.cit.*; p.177.

Gothicists as well as polychromatic detailing by using stones of contrast-
ing colors. Second, Gothic Revival required dynamic architectural sculpture and decoration. This became possible when John Lockwood Kipling
was hired as a professor of Architectural Sculpture at the Bombay School
of Art in 1865.[19] Under the supervision of Kipling, students at the Bombay
School began to make marble, stone, and plaster decorations for many
of the public buildings that were coming up in Bombay and Poona. As
Mahrukh Tarapor has noted "Their decorations were particularly note-
worthy for introducing natural forms into much architectural ornament
in India's official edifices, an innovation."[20] John Griffiths (1838–1918),
teacher of decorative painting, for example, led a group of students in the
decorations of the High Court and Victoria Terminus buildings. Partha
Mitter observed that "In the decoration of public buildings in Bombay
under Kipling, students enjoyed giving 'play to the grotesque and the
fanciful common to Indian and Mediaeval art.'"[21]

*Fig. 22: Mumbai, Taj Mahal Hotel (1903) in the
1920s.*

The Taj Mahal Hotel, Bombay.

19   Stamp, Gavin, "British Architecture in India, 1857–1947", *Journal of the Royal Society of Arts*, 1981/129; p. 363.

20   Tarapor, Mahrukh, "John Lockwood Kipling and British Art in India," *Victorian
Studies* 24, Indiana University Press, 1980/64; p.53-81.

21   Mitter, Partha, *Art and Nationalism in Colonial India, 1850–1922*, Cambridge,
Cambridge University Press, 1994; p. 61.

Apollo Bunder is located at the southern end of the north-south axis, which is the location of the Indian industrialist Jamsetji N. Tata's (1839–1904) impressive and up-to-date Taj Mahal Hotel ("the Taj"), built in 1903, which became the city's premier hotel. Adjacent to it was the Green's Mansions, constructed in 1890 and purchased by the Tata Group by November 1904 to become the Green's Hotel ("Green's"), whose edge is on the right hand of the image.

Apollo Bunder, the Gateway to India

The Taj's towering central dome at a height of 240 feet is still used by the Indian Navy "as an official daytime triangulation point" [22] for its ships. Apollo Bunder was the main landing place for passengers until 1895 and a favourite place of resort for Bombay society during the colonial era. [23] It was also the place that one of the city's wealthy *shetias* might make their way to. Here were located the racially exclusive Bombay Yacht Club House (1881) to the east of the Apollo Bunder and the Royal Bombay Yacht Club Chambers (1895–1897) where natives were only welcome as employees. In contrast, the Taj and Green's was open to members of all races. Foregrounding these structures was the final colonial monument built here in 1927, the Gateway of India, designed by George Wittet, to mark the place where king-emperor, George V, and Queen Mary, first stepped ashore in 1911. [24] Tata's biographer stated that the impetus behind this hotel was Tata's "patriotism and love for the city," [25] but a common Bombay tale is that Tata was denied entry into the dining hall of Watson's Esplanade Hotel and vowed to build a grander hotel where Indians would not face discrimination. This story is not considered to be true, but it has

---

22   URL: https://www.tajhotels.com/en-in/taj/taj-mahal-palace-mumbai/stories/ (02.02.2023).

23   Maclean, *op.cit.*; p. 205.

24   Morris, Jan; Winchester, Simon, *Stones of Empire: The Buildings of the Raj*, London, Oxford University Press, 1983; p.194-95.

25   Harris, F.R., *Jamsetji Nusserwanji Tata: A Chronicle of His Life*, London, Oxford University Press, 1925; p. 77–80.

survived because it seems like a case where the Empire strikes back, even though only the very wealthy could afford to patronize the hotel.

The Taj and Green's interrupted the racially exclusive enclaves of the Yacht Club, to create a middle-ground where the city's English-speaking native elite interacted with colonial officials, Indian politicians, expatriates, exiled artists, and many others. The Taj and Green's were important venues for jazz, and the art scene, including figures associated with the Progressives. Rachel Lee makes the case that "The Taj and Green's were key sites in the public cultural and social life of Bombay's educated English-speaking elites. Both hotels were contact zones that enabled the paths and social lives of travelers, locals, exiles and migrants to intersect."[26]

Seeking inspiration for the design of his own house, the Esplanade House, and the Taj, Tata toured the world for architectural ideas and equipment to make sure that these buildings were modern, stylistically eclectic, and yet personal. For the design of the Taj, Tata had very particular ideas and worked with Raosaheb Sitaram Khanderao Vaidya, who had overseen the construction of the Sailors' Home, and D.N. Mirza. Following Vaidya's demise in 1900, W.A. Chambers, representing the firm Gostling, Chambers & Fritchley, became the architect. Both Vaidya and Chambers had previously worked with Stevens on his Gothic Revival public buildings. While maintaining much of the original design, Chambers altered the shape of the central dome. The hotel's website proudly discusses its eclectic range of influences: "With its Indo-Saracenic arches and distinctive, red-tiled Florentine gothic dome, carved with Victorian Gothic and Romanesque details along with Edwardian touches on the roof, it is truly an architectural jewel."[27] The

26   Lee, Rachel, "Hospitable Environments: The Taj Mahal Hotel and green's Hotel as site of cultural production in Bombay", in: Dogramaci et al. (eds.), *Arrival Cities. Migrating Artists and New Metropolitan Topographies in the 20th Century*, Leuven, Leuven University Press, 2020. Open access: https://lup.be/products/1 32128 (01.02.2023). For a definition of "contact zone": see Pratt Mary Louise, *Imperial Eyes: Travel Writing and Transculturation*, London, Routledge, 1992; p. 6–7.

27   Dwivedi, Sharada; Mehrotra, Rahul, *Fort Walks: Around Bombay's Fort Area*, Mumbai, Eminence, 1999; p.47. Quote from hotel website: https://www.tajhote

building defies any stylistic definition with its large central dome and four onion shaped cupolas at the corners. Its *jharokha* like projecting balconies resemble those from Mughal or Rajput architecture and yet often have tiled roofs, and arch types used vary from the Gothic pointed to semi-circular. It was a Parsi contractor, Sorabji Contractor who constructed the building and conceived of the well-known cantilevered central staircase.

The nationalist spirit animated the policies of the Parsi industrialist Jamsetji Nusserwanji Tata (1839–1904), who was instrumental in establishing educational scholarships for Indian students to pursue their higher studies abroad and sought to find a Scientific Research Institute.[28] This shows Tata aimed to nurture native expertise. Tata's biographer, D.E. Wacha has described him as "a Swadeshi of Swadeshists long before Swadeshism was boomed in Bengal."[29] Swadeshi refers to something made or manufactured within one's own country. When he planned a new mill in Bombay in 1886, he called it the "Swadeshi Mills." Tata's plan was to compete with Lancashire to spin finer yarn and produce finer cloth to substantially reduce imports, a version of swadeshi.[30] The Swadeshi movement of Bengal of 1905 asked Indians to boycott foreign goods and buy domestic products. One might think of the Taj as a version of swadeshi, where the Tata used Indian and western expertise to construct a hotel which prides itself for coming "with many firsts": the country's "first hotel to have electricity, American fans, German elevators, Turkish baths and English butlers."[31] Confidently naming the hotel after the Taj Mahal, signaled its excellence. If

---

ls.com/en-in/taj/taj-mahal-palace-mumbai/stories/. The website includes the name of D. N. Mirza but does not mention W. A. Chambers (01.02.2023).

28   Wacha Edulji, Dinshaw, *The Life & Work of J. N. Tata*, Madras, Ganesh & Co., 1915; p.11. For Tata scholarships, see https://www.tatatrusts.org/our-work/individual-grants-programme/education-grants. I am also a former recipient of a J. N. Tata Endowment loan scholarship.

29   *Ibid.*; p. 8.

30   *Ibid.*; p. 8–9.

31   See   https://www.tajhotels.com/en-in/taj/taj-mahal-palace-mumbai/stories/ (01.02.2023).

the British picked and chose elements from Indian architecture in the making of Indo-Saracenic architecture, or in the detailing of their buildings, Tata felt free to pick and choose from the world's architecture. The significance of Tata's projects is that they herald a spirit of independence from colonialism. Seeking and incorporating ideas for architecture and technology from India, and abroad in Europe, Tata provincialized the colonial regime by his self-sufficiency, by simply by not requiring their guidance.

Fig. 23: Mumbai, Taj Mahal Hotel and Taj Mahal Tower, model of the 1970s.

It was on the steps of the Taj Mahal Hotel and not a government building that Lord Mountbatten made the announcement of India's independence in 1947. Over two decades after India's independence, in 1973, The Taj Mahal Tower, a business hotel, was opened, taking the place of Green's Hotel. Melton Bekker, an American architect, envisioned its L-shaped structure, while Rustam Patell, is credited "as the architect and designer" who brought this vision to fruition. Bekker also borrowed from unrelated Indian architectural traditions, including pillars from Tanjore in the south, "arched balconies from Rajasthan into [sic] the distinctive tower which is crowned with a jagged diadem."[32] The tower rises from an arcaded podium that echoes the arcade at the ground floor of the Taj. On the Arabian sea-facing façade, the tower's edges on either side form a vertical band that include two arched windows that are setback slightly to frame the tower, while the upper flower with large windows cantilevers out like a crown. As the painted image reveals, the wide-spreading Taj with its central dome still dominates the scene, with the Taj Tower as a vertical accent. Beyond, one is made aware of the rising, less luxurious cityscape.

Heritage and decolonization

The collection of postcards compels me to return once again to the site of Flora Fountain in the post-independence period. After India's independence in 1947, the multilingual city of Bombay's future was caught up in debates from the late 1940s and 1950s over the establishment of linguistic states within India. In November 1955, there was a proposal to carve three states out of Bombay state with the city of Bombay as one. Protesting the three-state solution, a large procession against this proposal resulted in the killing of protestors by the police near Flora Fountain in 1955. This came to be seen as a pivotal moment in the battle for Samyukta Maharashtra (United Maharashtra). Those who died here and were killed by the police in 1956, came to be seen "as 'martyrs [*hutatma*]' for their homeland." The Samyukta Maharashtra Samiti (SMS) formed in 1956 were important in representing the interests of Marathi speakers (versus Gujarati speakers) in leading the fight against the three-state solution. Before the division of Bombay state into Maharashtra and Gujarat on 1 May 1960, the SMS led a torchlight procession to Flora Fountain where a memorial pillar had been raised. A foundation stone of the martyr's memorial was laid the next year. Officially, the name of this space was changed to Hutatma Chowk (Martyrs' Square), and government ceremonies ensure its continued importance in sub-national

---

32   *Ibid.*

nationalism, that is, patriotism towards Maharashtra. A tall pillar holds up a bronze sculpture of a farmer and worker who together hold a torch and slab, which has etched into it, the names of 105 martyrs.[33] This is also a memorial that reminds us of the violence of the police and the state against its citizens in the postcolonial era, where the tensions of nationalism still simmer after independence. The postcards show us Hutatma Chowk with the fountain and memorial bound together in the center of the parking lot, with both identities existing. One image shows us the outlines of the parking spaces, while the other emphasizes the parked cars and the traffic dense traffic here.

Fig. 24: Mumbai, Flora Fountain in the 1960s.

As "Floral Fountain" became "Flora Fountain" another history became possible, and scholars have incorrectly shown that the fountain is part of the larger history of the Jews in India.[34] Rather than a Roman goddess, scholars point out that the fountain is named after the renowned Flora

---

33   Isaka, Riho, "The multilingual city of Bombay and the formation of linguistic states, 1947–60," in: Bates Crispin, Mio Minoru (eds.), *Cities in South Asia*, New York, Routledge, 2015; p. 143–158.

34   See, for example, Joan G., Roland, "The Baghdadi Jews," in: Slapak, Orpa (ed.), *The Jews of India: A Story of Three Communities*, Jerusalem, Israel Museum, 1995;

Sassoon (1859–1936), famous for her good judgement in business, charity, philanthropy, and her piety as a Jew. Widow of Solomon Sassoon
(1841–1894), and daughter-in-law of David Sassoon (1793–1864), the
legendary founder of this illustrious Baghdadi Jewish family in Bombay
of merchants and industrialists. While Solomon is credited with making
the family's commercial enterprises global, after his death Flora "truly
internationalized the family businesses and she continued its philan-
thropic endeavours." She also facilitated the family's slow transfer to
London, not long after the early twentieth century. Apparently, "Bom-
bayites remember her today, thanks to the dominant Flora Fountain
near Victoria Station."[35] The Flora Fountain is part of a Jewish itinerary
in Bombay, which could start from the Gateway of India, that was also
financed partially by a member of the Sassoon family. In 2017, as Flora
Fountain was being restored, conservation architect Vikas Dilawari and
the structural engineers working with him first uncovered the fountain's
underground water network because they wanted to understand what
had stopped the flow of water through the outlets on the mouths of fish
on the fountain and restore the system. Apparently, a well, which is now
underground is the source of the fountain's water and has been restored.
Perhaps, in reference to the well, "Flora Fountain" is also referred to as
"Mulji Jetha Pyau," possibly the name of the donor of the well.[36] Flora
Fountain, this urban junction, is truly the fountain that keeps giving!

    p.37-46; Silliman, Jael, *Jewish Portraits, Indian Frames: Women's Narratives from a
    Diaspora of Hope*, Hanover, Brandeis, 2003.

35   Katz, Nathan, *Who are the Jews of India?*, Berkeley, University of California Press,
    2000; p. 141.

36   Vartak, Priyanka, "Mumbai: Flora Fountain restoration makes architect 'dig'
    deep into history," *Free Press Journal*, Mumbai.

References

AD Staff, "World Heritage Day: Mumbai's Flora Fountain to see light of day this December," 19 April 2018, https://www.architecturaldigest.in/content/flora-fountain-fort-mumbai-restoration/(accessed 05.02.2023).

Anonymous, "Anglo-Indian Architecture," *Builder* 55 (3 November 1888); p. 313–15.

Baucom, Ian, *Out of Place: Englishness, Empire, and the Locations of Identity*, Princeton, NJ, Princeton University Press, 1999.

Butler, Samuel, *Erewhon or, Over the Range*, New York, Modern Library, 1872.

Davies, Philip, *Splendours of The Raj: British Architecture in India 1660–1947*, Harmondsworth, Penguin Books, 1985.

Dwivedi, Sharada; Mehrotra, Rahul, *Fort Walks: Around Bombay's Fort Area*, Mumbai, Eminence Designs Pvt. Ltd., 1999.

Edwardes, S. M. (compiler), *The Gazetteer of Bombay City and Island*, 3 vols., Bombay, Times Press, 1909–1910.

Furneaux, J. H., *Glimpses of India: A Grand Photographic History of The Land of Antiquity, the vast Empire of the East*, Bombay, C. B. Burrows, 1895.

Green, Nile, *Bombay Islam: The Religious Economy of the West Indian Ocean 1840–1915*, Cambridge, Cambridge University Press, 2011.

Harris, F.R., *Jamsetji Nusserwanji Tata: A Chronicle of His Life*, London, Oxford University Press, 1925.

Isaka, Riho, "The multilingual city of Bombay and the formation of linguistic states, 1947–60," in: Bates, Crispin; Mio, Minoru (eds.), *Cities in South Asia*, New York, Routledge, 2015; p. 143–158.

Katz, Nathan, *Who are the Jews of India?*, Berkeley, University of California Press, 2000.

Lee, Rachel, "Hospitable Environments: The Taj Mahal Hotel and Green's Hotel as Sites of Cultural Production in Bombay," in: Dogramaci, Burcu; Hetschold, Mareike; Karp Lugo, Laura; Lee, Rachel; Roth, Helen (eds.), *Arrival Cities: Migrating Artists and New Metropolitan Topographies in the 20th Century*, Leuven, Leuven University Press, 2020; p. 249–268.

Mackenzie Maclean, James, *A Guide to Bombay: Historical, Statistical, and Descriptive*, fourteenth edition, Bombay, Bombay Gazette Steam Press, 1889.

Mackenzie Maclean, James. *A Guide to Bombay. Historical, Statistical, and Descriptive*, 31st ed., Bombay, Bombay Gazette Steam Press, 1906.

Mehrotra, Rahul, "Bazaars in Victorian Arcades: Conserving Bombay's Historic Core," in: Dandekar, Hemalata (ed.), *City Space + Globalization: An International Perspective*, 1998, https://digitalcommons.calpol y.edu/books_fac/3/; p. 46–53.

Mitter, Partha, *Art and Nationalism in Colonial India, 1850–1922*, Cambridge, Cambridge University Press, 1994.

Morris, Jan; Winchester, Simon, *Stones of Empire: The Buildings of the Raj*, Oxford, Oxford University Press, 1983.

Murzban, Muncherji, *Leaves from the Life of Khan Bahadur Muncherji Cowasji Murzban, C. I. E.: With an Introduction Containing a Life-Sketch of Fardunji Murzbanji*, Bombay, printed for author by Furdoonji Byramji Marzban, 1915.

"Our Story: The Taj Mahal Palace, Mumbai," https://www.tajhotels.com /en-in/taj/taj-mahal-palace-mumbai/stories/ (05.02.2023).

Oxford English Dictionary (OED), second edition (1989), https://www.o ed.com/oed2/00169695 (05.02.2023).

Pratt, Mary Louise, *Imperial Eyes: Travel Writing and Transculturation*, London, Routledge, 1992.

Roland, Joan G., "The Baghdadi Jews," in: Slapak, Orpa (ed.), *The Jews of India: A Story of Three Communities*, Jerusalem, Israel Museum, 1995; p. 37–46.

Silliman, Jael, *Jewish Portraits, Indian Frames: Women's Narratives from a Diaspora of Hope*, Hanover, NH, University Press of New England, 2003.

Stamp, Gavin, "British Architecture in India, 1857–1947," *Journal of the Royal Society of Arts*, 1981/129; p. 357–379.

"Taj Mahal Tower, Mumbai," https://www.tajhotels.com/en-in/taj/taj-m ahal-tower-mumbai/ (accessed 05.02.2023).

Tarapor, Mahrukh, "John Lockwood Kipling and British Art in India," *Victorian Studies* 1980/24; p. 53–81.

"Tata Trusts: Our work," https://www.tatatrusts.org/our-work/individu
al-grants-programme/education-grants, (05.02.2023).

Vartak, Priyanka, "Mumbai: Flora Fountain restoration makes architect
'dig' deep into history," *Free Press Journal*, Mumbai (June 19, 2017),ht
tps://ezproxy.library.wisc.edu/login?url=https://www.proquest.co
m/magazines/mumbai-flora-fountain-restoration-makes-architec
t/docview/2290265377/se-2?accountid=465 (05.02.2023).

Wacha, Edulji Dinshaw, *The Life & Work of J. N. Tata*, second edition,
Madras, Ganesh & Co., 1915.

Delhi—Beyond its 'appearance'

Anupam Bansal

Cities across the world are identifiable through their images, particularly of its iconic architecture. Delhi is no different. With varied layers overlapping in Delhi's political and cultural history, each era has left its indelible mark on the face of the City. Iconic images of Qutub Minar, the Humayun's Tomb, Rashtrapati Bhawan (former Viceregal Palace), Kartavya Path (Former Raj Path and Kingsway) or modern icons such as the Ashoka Hotel, Claridges Hotel etc. have formed the imagination of Delhi in people's mind particularly those who have not visited the city.

Fig. 25: New Delhi, Connaught Place (1933) in the 1960s.

The postcard collection sent by European travellers from India scattered among collectors all over Europe formed the starting point for this essay. The collection reflects the choices made by the visitors sometimes on a professional trip, sometimes young people on a "hippie trail". These photos capture the 'appearance' of the city. It is ironic that these images seem frozen in time particularly when viewed from the context of a city which has expanded or rather exploded in the last 40 years.

The lived experience of Delhi has altered immensely from a sleepy political capital to a fast-transforming megapolis. It is projected that Delhi will overtake Tokyo as the most populated urban agglomeration by 2028. Most of the expansion in Delhi has occurred on the peripheries as rural areas have become more urban and densification of existing unplanned areas in the core, which lack proper development control regulations.[1] The geographic size of Delhi has more than doubled from 624.28 sq. km.[1] in 1991 to 1483 Sq. km. in 2011.[2] Since Economic Liberalisation in 1991, the population has doubled, from 8.4 million[3] to an estimated 19 million today. Delhi has grown from being a political capital to a business hub and a magnet of urban migration. People have moved to the city to find jobs, for education and other newly available opportunities. But residential space to accommodate them, at least planned space, has been scarce. The Delhi Development Authority's (DDA) planned development has severely failed to keep pace with migration and economic changes occurring in the city.

This housing gap is disproportionately skewed in the low-income segment, therefore poorer migrants often retort to being accommodated in the low-income settlements such as unauthorised colonies, urban villages or slum clusters.

---

1   Dupont, Véronique, *Spatial and Demographic Growth of Delhi since 1947 and the Main Migration Flows*, Institut de recherche pour le Developpement, Paris, 2000, URL: https://www.researchgate.net/publication/282170328_Spatial_an d_demographic_growth_of_Delhi_since_1947_and_the_main_migration_flo ws (15.02.2023).

2   Census of India, 2011.

3   Dupont, *op.cit.*

Fig. 26: New Delhi, Parliament House (1927) in the
1960s.

Fig. 27: New Delhi, All India Radio (1936) in the
1960s.

"The development of land and housing in Delhi has largely been the
prerogative of the public sector, with limited private participation.
Such processes have not kept pace with the growing demand for
housing. The high cost of land in the city has also resulted in making
housing unaffordable." [4]

---

4   Draft Master Plan Delhi (MPD) 2041; p. 50.

As a result of the widening gap between the rate of migration and rate of development of planned housing, several types of housing settlements have evolved, mostly outside the ambit of the Master Plan and other legal provisions. Colonies, Jhuggi Jhopri Clusters (Squatter Settlements), planned Low Income Group or Economically Weaker Sections Housing and many more form a complex web of settlement patterns in the city. Instead of the periphery, or squatter settlements on the urban edge, the influx of migrants has permeated in the oldest settlements of the city, the so-called *Lal-Dora (Red Line)[5]* areas or "Urban Villages", where new forms of rental housing have emerged. These enclaves bear the brunt of urbanization and have transformed both socially and physically.

Settlement types

In its report on cities of Delhi, the Centre for Policy Research has classified (as originally classified by policy and planning documents) eight types of settlement in Delhi, only one of which is termed "planned". The other seven types of settlement become, by opposition, 'unplanned'. This 'unplanned' city houses the vast majority of Delhi's residents across the economic spectrum: these settlements include both the affluent farmhouses of South Delhi, which are well-built colonies populated by successful businesspeople, and 700+ dense slum-like areas spread across the city. Only an estimated 23% of the population of Delhi resides in the so-called planned settlements.[6]

This essay depicts the character of the grain of the city rather than its iconic. It presents a day-to-day reality of the city rather than its *'appearance'* captured in tourist postcards. Vasant Kunj, a large, planned colony

---

5   The land earmarked for village abadi (land and building inhabited by villagers) and the agricultural land of the village were duly demarcated in the land settlement of 1908–09 and the abadi site was circumscribed in the village map in red ink. That is how it came to be commonly known as Lal Dora.

6   Centre for Policy Research, *Categorisation of Settlement in Delhi*, Mai 2015, http s://cprindia.org/project/cities-of-delhi/ (15.02.2023).

in S-W Delhi is studied as a spatial transect rather than a single neighbourhood or housing typology because this type of spatial analysis allows for a picture of Delhi that demonstrate the ways in which the formal and the informal, the authorized and the unauthorised, and the planned and the unplanned coexist. Outside of Lutyens Delhi,[7] any such transect will reveal a similar cross-section of settlement and housing types. For this essay, Vasant Kunj is referred to as a geographical extent extending approximately 7 km between the Mahipalpur Village on the West and Mehrauli on the Eastern edge.

Vasant Kunj as a spatial transect

Vasant Kunj was developed in the late 1970s as a residential area by DDA to address the growing housing needs of the city. The construction of the first phase of the housing was completed in the 1980s. It was largely developed on agricultural land acquired by DDA from farmers residing in Mahipalpur, Masoodpur and Kishangarh villages. The visual study conducted through google maps illustrated here reveals at least 4 distinct settlements; it highlights both the spatial diversity and inequality that exists in these various settlement types.

Planned—DDA Housing
The first settlement identifiable by its grid-like geometric layout of apartments arranged in vast open green spaces are the "planned colonies" in Vasant Kunj, primarily developed by DDA. Planned colonies are also referred to as "approved" colonies. These settlements sit on land demarcated as "development area" in the Master Plan of Delhi. At the time of construction, housing units in these colonies comply with planning norms and are fully serviced with infrastructure such as water

---

7   Lutyens' Delhi is an area in New Delhi, named after the British architect Sir
     Edwin Lutyens (1869–1944), who was responsible for much of the city planning
     and architectural design during the period of the British Raj, when India was
     part of the British Empire in the 1920s.

pipelines and sewerage systems. The housing constructed by the Delhi Development Authority (DDA) exemplifies this category of settlement.[8] Vasant Kunj is divided into five sectors numbered from A to E. Each sector is treated as an individual colony with its own services and facilities such as markets, schools, and recreational facilities. Often arranged in blocks of sixteen dwellings: four storeys with four units per floor. While some of the blocks of four are joined to the adjacent ones, the others have passages between them for the service pipes and infrastructure. These passages alternately widen to allow movement through them.

DDA housing in Vasant Kunj (like other parts of Delhi) are characterized by flat roofs, external surfaces finished in plain plaster with cement or lime wash, with functional sunshades providing the only relief to an otherwise bland facade. It has often been criticised for its repetitiveness and 'rubber stamp' architecture. Though utilitarian modern to start with, most apartments have acquired a unique character that has been shaped by individual owners particularly in their remodelled interior layouts. Almost all the sectors built in Vasant Kunj consist of four storeys walk up apartments as lifts were considered very expensive during the time these were built. Providing open space in the form of parks, tot-lots for children were the prime considerations for design. This idea permeated the design of typologies as well; terraces, balconies and accessible roofs were provided as a response to the Indian lifestyle where people often slept outdoors in the absence of air conditioning. The dwelling units provided residents with ample space on all floors to sleep outside. When initially built only scooter parkings were provided in colonies. Post Liberalization in 1991, and with a proliferation of private car ownership, today there is a severe shortage of parking spaces, sometimes even leading to neighbourly discord.

---

8   Centre for Policy Research, 2015; *op. cit.*

Urban Villages—Kishangarh, Masoodpur & Mahipalpur

"Urban Villages" are the second type of settlements, identifiable through their narrow streets, densely built fabric and lack of open spaces. The word 'urban village' holds a unique meaning in Delhi. First used in the Master Plan it applies to villages whose *abadi* (Land and building inhabited by villagers) areas are within the urbanizable limits. Once the entire region surrounding the village is urbanized and no rural livelihoods are continued, the village is declared as an urban. Upon declaration as "urban", the *"Lal Dora"* area in a village ceases to exist and the provisions of the Master Plan, Zonal Plan, or relevant Area Development Plan and Building Byelaws become applicable. Agriculture lands of Masoodpur, Kishangarh and Mahipalpur villages were taken over by DDA soon after Master Plan I (1962) and they became part of urban Delhi (when Vasant Kunj flats had been partially constructed) around 1985. Locals were paid Rs. 1.70 per sq. Yards as price for their land.[9] Now listed as urban villages under the municipality, these villages have transformed from a few hundred households with one dominant caste to many thousands of households and a mix of tenants from multiple regions of the country. This reflects the lack of availability of planned housing for the poor in the city.

Almost four decades after their acquisition, each village has acquired its distinctive image and economy depending upon its location and emerging needs in the city. Mahipalpur has emerged as a hotel enclave owing to its proximity to the Delhi Airport. Masoodpur is characterized by retail shops mostly catering to the needs of Vasant Kunj residents and its dairy farm which continues to supply milk to the surrounding areas

---

9   Interview with Mr. Rattan Singh, resident of Kishangarh Village whose father had sold land to DDA and received compensation in return. He remembered how his childhood was spent helping his father in farming. After his father sold their land, he took up a government job, and retired from the TATA company. While he was barely educated until high school, his children were educated and practicing professionals. He owed this transformation to development of Kishangarh as a result of development of Vasant Kunj.

to this day. Kishangarh has largely transformed into Rental housing for the migrant populace. Kishangarh was settled around 150–200 years back when the farming Jats from Mehrauli moved to their field slowly by establishing *chappar* (small huts). They were however dependent on Mehrauli for their daily needs and to sell their grain and crops in Mehrauli *mandis* (wholesale markets). Children from the village used to walk to Mehrauli to attend school as well. Mahipalpur on the Western edge of Vasant Kunj, close to the IGI Airport is a historic village located north of the Mehrauli-Mahipalpur road and east of NH-8 in the area where the north-south ridge and the southern east-west ridge meet. In the 14th century Feroze Shah Tughlaq had built here a hunting lodge (which still exists) and a *bundh* (embankment) to retain rainwater flowing from surrounding hilly mounds. Close to the Mahipalpur towards the Southeast also lies the historic site of Sultan Garhi, built in 13th Century by Sultan Iltutmish. In the past two decades, Mahipalpur has emerged as Delhi's largest hotel hub after Paharganj. The Jat-dominated village, which once had warehouses, factory outlets, and car workshops, today boasts of more than 150 hotels, half of them owned by villagers, who proudly term themselves farmers-turned-hoteliers. Most villagers who run hotels continue to live in the locality but with new lifestyles: there are many who have switched from motorcycle to Mercedes in a few years. Among the new residents of this village are youngsters working in Aerocity, the Delhi airport and Gurgaon. It is not unusual to see young men and women working with airlines walking in the streets of the village in uniform. Masoodpur village is located midway between Kishangarh & Mahipalpur. Its settlement area was on the north, while cattle sheds of some families and common grasslands were on the south of the road. The village had more than 300 households. At its center was the old *chaupal* (village community space), which had a tree with sitting space around till 2006 and is now a concrete hall structure; an ancestral shrine that is worshipped by all castes in the village is to the west. The common well is on the north edge; adjacent to it was a rain-fed water pond (johar) now a DDA park, further north is the cremation ground. To the east along the road are commons, which house a community centre.

The economy of these villages apart from other income sources like hotels in Mahipalpur, retail shops and dairy in Masoodpur are largely dependent on rental income. They provide cheap residences catering to diverse income groups ranging from professionals, educated migrants and domestic workers who cannot afford the steep South Delhi rents. The villages are now characterized by five to six storey buildings. These buildings are owned and managed by Jat landlords who converted their two-storey houses into multi-storey buildings to lease to migrants from north and eastern India. They invest the rent collected from these tenements in the real estate market on the outskirts of the city. These buildings have largely come up in the last two decades after Liberalisation. As buildings above 15m height are classified as "High Rise" as per the National Building Code of India, making it mandatory to meet requirements for fire safety, majority of the new buildings in the villages limit within 15m height. However, it is not uncommon to find buildings that do not comply and brazenly flout fire safety norms.

At the time these villages were notified, the bulk of houses in the villages were 'havelis'. The term haveli usually referred to private mansions in North India, which would contain one or more courtyards. While some havelis were rather elaborate with as many as four or five floors, the common ones existing in the by lanes of these villages were rather modest with a row of rooms interjected by a courtyard in the centre. Scattered in the numerous galis (lanes), the havelis had similar architectural features such as darwaza (gateway with an ornate wooden door) angan (courtyard), tehkhana (underground chamber) deori (raised plinth). The deori ensured privacy and prevented ingress of water during the monsoon season. It was common for most havelis to be constructed with stone or brick masonry, with roofs made of stone slabs supported with wooden rafters. Toilets were not inside houses, and everyone had to go to grasslands. Washing water was drawn from the well by women and stored in the common wash area. Today it is difficult to find surviving havelis as most of them have been demolished and replaced by 4–5 storey concrete and brick buildings usually with typical units plans stacked over each other. The houses had started moving vertical about 20–30 years ago after the 4 storey DDA flats came up in the area. The most intensive construction came after 1995 when most houses were replaced with multi-storeyed buildings.

Jhuggi Jhopri Cluster (JJC)–Rangpuri

The third type of settlement in Vasant Kunj, identifiable by the small size of houses, temporary materials of construction, lack of proper roads and services are the "Jhuggi Jhopri Clusters (JJC)" These slum settlements have continued to grow and expand across Delhi. These non-notified slums are categorised as Jhuggi Jhopri Clusters (JJCs). These are defined as "squatter settlements" located on "public land"—land owned by any government agency—which has been occupied and built on without permission. As a result, these settlements are often referred to as "encroachments" in official discourse.[10] Rangpuri Pahari is one such settlement located west of Vasant Kunj Flats or it is more accurate to describe Vasant Kunj as the area east of Rangpuri Pahari, (which has been there long before). Quarrying of stone ('pahar') in the area started in the '50s. Depending upon specific locations in the area and demographic profile of their residents different names have evolved such Rangpuri Pahari Malakpur Kohi, Rangpuri Pahari Nala, Rangpuri Pahari Sarak Paar and Israil Camp.

A fair amount of Delhi's 'planned development' including its airport is made out of stone quarried from Rangpuri Pahari. These settlements were of workers who quarried this stone when needed, broke it into various sizes and transported it until the quarries were closed pursuant to Supreme Court directions. Even now, especially in Malakpur Kohi and Nala, most families are of quarry workers. Being a stone's throw from the sprawling Indra Gandhi International airport and not far from the gleaming business district of Gurgaon, it is typical of the fringes of India's national capital. It sits amidst the dusty landscape, in what were once low-lying hills before the scramble for urban growth consumed the area. Today, the surroundings have been reduced to a dumping ground for construction waste and litter. Tarpaulin tents and makeshift cabins, lining narrow alleys, make up the settlement and house the residents.

---

10   Centre for Policy Research; *op. cit.*

Unauthorized Colony—Green Avenue

The last type of settlement in Vasant Kunj are the "Unauthorized Colonies". The character of Unauthorized colonies can vary from a dense settlement like Sangam Vihar to sparsely populated Sainik Farms (both in South Delhi). Unauthorised colonies are built in contravention of zoning regulations, developed either in violation of Delhi's Master Plan or on 'illegally' subdivided agricultural land. The literature on unauthorised colonies sets out two distinguishing features: one, these areas have been 'illegally' subdivided into plots, and; two, the buyers of plots in these settlements posses documents (mostly in the form of a general power of attorney or GPA) that prove some form of tenure, which may be characterised as 'semi-legal'. In recent years, the government has introduced a policy framework for regularisation of these colonies, a process designed to bring these settlements into the legal ambit.[11] According to the current official estimates there are 1700+ unauthorised colonies in Delhi housing more than 5 million inhabitants. Ironically the unauthorized colonies are not restricted to housing the urban poor or the migrant population. Farmhouses for the most affluent of Delhi's population occupying about 3500 hectares of agricultural land also constitute "Unauthorized Colonies". Owned by the elites of Delhi, these enclaves have brought profound changes in the size of land holdings, spatial shifts in agricultural practices and changes in land values.

Located on SE fringe of Vasant Kunj, the farmhouses of Green Avenue occupies a large area characterized by high security walls, gates and palatial villas amidst lush and verdant landscape. Typically, farmhouses are large and luxurious amidst spacious and green surroundings. These farmhouses comprise a large plot of land ranging from 1 to 5 acres having enough space for a large house, a garden and other amenity. Usually, the houses are built with high-quality (expensive and modern) materials and have several bedrooms, living, dining areas along with a large kitchen etc. High boundary walls around the plot (owing to privacy and

11   *Ibid.*

safety issues), Large windows and balconies that offer views of the surrounding greens characterize the luxury houses. Majority of these may consist of a garden or a lawn along with an outdoor swimming pool with a deck or a patio. Additionally, these farmhouses would also have a range of amenities like a gym, home theatre, play area for children and servant's quarters depending upon the personal preferences and the budget of the owner. The architecture of the farmhouses varies from Colonial, Neoclassical, Traditional to Modern and minimal.

Current challenges—Ecological / Unsafe Buildings in Villages / Unsanitary living conditions of JJC

Though only four settlement types are illustrated in the essay, a microscopic view will reveal further gradation of housing types. It is common to find overlap of different types within the confines of the identified settlements. Unauthorized constructions are rampant in Urban Villages. Many smaller examples of JJCs like Arjun camp, Masjid Compound are found in interstitial spaces or along roads and undeveloped land. The only strong connection between the disparate settlements is the Vasant Kunj Road. Other connections and linkages between planned sectors or between planned, urban villages, JJC are almost non-existent. The DDA master plan developed each sector as an independent unit and virtually without any links with the other settlements. Thus, the overall experience in Vasant Kunj is that of a fragmented and disjointed city. The mix of planned, dense, luxurious, and temporary forms an unexceptional urban form, it lacks a vocabulary to satisfactorily describe it. This urban form and its organizing principles are hard to decipher. Further scholarly inquiry is required to map and document the complex pattern of built form as well as the socio-cultural aspect of their residents.

The frenzied pace of development in the last 3–4 decades has rendered the once rural landscapes unrecognizable and transformed. Remnants of the past both built and natural have been erased. A closer look at the water bodies in and around Vasant Kunj gives an idea of the ecological transformation. The traditional water bodies and the drainage channels have faced the onslaught of urbanization. The village pond of Kishangarh next to Baba Laturia Temple built with ghats is all but bone dry now. The pond now gets only a few inches of water during the monsoons. Barely about 30 years ago, the entire village's cattle came here to slake their thirst. Barely a kilometer from the Kishangarh Village Pond is Machali (Fish) Park named after a thriving population of Cat Fish found in its lake where water runoff from Mehrauli is still collected. This is one of the only surviving lakes in the area owing to its location in a popular park as well as good maintenance and upkeep by DDA. On the other end of Kishangarh Village, the extremely picturesque lake known as the Neela Hauz was almost killed for widening the road into four-lanes in the run up to the Commonwealth Games in 2010. The residents of Vasant Kunj, through a citizen's initiative were able to intervene in a timely manner to partially save the lake. However, the fate of village ponds of Masoodpur and Mahipalpur has been of utter neglect and apathy. The Masoodpur lake has been converted to a DDA park while the development of Vasant Kunj has completely disrupted the watershed of the Mahipalpur bundh (embankment). The built environment in the urban villages is considered unsafe as a result of a combination of factors, including population growth, inadequate planning and investment.

These villages are densely populated, leading to overcrowding. People live in cramped and poorly ventilated spaces. Lacking basic service infrastructure such as proper sanitation facilities, clean water supply, and waste management systems result in unsanitary conditions. Often constructed with low-quality materials and poor workmanship, buildings in these villages are often vulnerable to collapse and other safety hazards. Most buildings lack proper fire safety measures, such as fire escapes, smoke detectors, and fire extinguishers. Narrow access roads limit access of emergency vehicles. In addition, residents of these villages have limited access to green spaces, which can contribute to a lack of fresh air and recreation opportunities for residents. Residents of Rangpuri Pahari's (JJC) access to basic services and social security programs is practically non-existent, services too are scarce. Due to lack of identification documents the residents remain out of many services and social security benefits—most of which are now linked to biometric identification processes. Lacking access to primary education, young boys often labour on construction sites or occasionally fall back on traditional occupations, such as drumming at wedding ceremonies. The girls, on the other hand, help with domestic chores and join their mothers as rag-pickers or domestic help in the houses of the middle-class families in apartment blocks nearby. However, close they might be to the engines of growth these communities lack secure habitation, only a small proportion of households have access to adequate sanitation, while health care and education are also out of reach for most of them. Most worryingly the residents face a constant threat of eviction from Government agencies.[12]

Future Trajectories and opportunities

The spatial diversity and housing differences within the settlements are striking. It is worthwhile to note that while the intended population of planned Vasant Kunj (100,000) has remained static, the population and density in the so-called villages, slum settlements and unauthorized colonies now exceed DDA sectors manyfold. The "Planned" sectors stand isolated as stagnant islands not able to transform or bear the pressures of urbanization.

The "*appearance*" of Vasant Kunj, is that of an urban fringe where recognizable signs of the city are barely visible as most sectors are setback from the roads and inconspicuous. If at all the city becomes perceptible where the road intersects with the villages of Kishangarh, Masoodpur and Mahipalpur. The chaos of buildings, shops and hawkers or as in the case of Mahipalpur, the hotels become recognizable symbols of urbanity. The writing of this essay coincided with my short stint as a reviewer for an Urban Design Studio where students were researching & mapping

---

12   Sajjad, Hassan, "*India: Living on the fringes of Delhi—the Ghiyaras of Rangpuri and their continued exclusion*", Minority Rights, 2018. URL: https://minorityrights.org/ programmes/library/trends/trends2018/india/ (15.02.2023).

the built environment of Vasant Kunj in order to project future scenarios of urban transformation. Two recent developments; i) the regeneration policy proposed in draft MPD 2041 and ii) commencement of Delhi Metro Phase IV construction were identified as key factors that will catalyze growth and Transformation in Vasant Kunj.

Fig. 28: Delhi, Map of Vasant Kunj.[13]

PLANNED COLONY   UNAUTHORIZED COLONY   JHUGGI JHOPRI CLUSTER (JJC)   URBAN VILLAGES

13   "Vasant Kunj is divided into five sectors (A-E). Each sector is treated as an individual colony with its own services and facilities such as markets, schools, and recreational facilities." (A. Bansal)

The draft Master Plan of Delhi-2041, has spelled out a "regeneration policy" for areas that have come up decades ago and now need better civic infrastructure. This regeneration or redevelopment policy will enable urban transformation and upgradation particularly in urbanised villages, unauthorised colonies, resettlement colonies, where redevelopment is the only way forward to improve the quality of life and built environment. The Phase IV Metro likely to be completed by December 2024 will enable Vasant Kunj residents to connect with the Airport and the rest of the city. It will also enhance connectivity within Vasant Kunj where public transport is minimal. It is expected to alter the skyline of Vasant Kunj particularly its Urban Villages that will be subject to further densification. As it continues to transform it is imperative to recognize the interdependence of the various settlements in Vasant Kunj. Though the majority of settlements may not qualify as "Planned" or "Authorized" the resultant urban fabric is vibrant and pluralistic as it provides for a varied section of population ranging from Ultra rich to the most marginalized poor. Each group is dependent on the other for its economic or functional needs.

References

Bansal, Anupam; Kochupillai, Malini (eds.), *Architectural Guide Delhi*, Berlin, DOM, 2013.

Census of India, 2011.

Centure for Policy Research, Categorisation of Stettlement in Delhi, Mai 2015.

Chakravarty, Surajit; Negi, Rohit (eds.), *Space, Planning and Everyday Contestations in Delhi*, New Delhi, Springer, 2016.

Delhi Development Authoriy, Draft Master Plan Delhi (MPD), 2041.

Dupont, Véronique, "Spatial and Demographic Growth of Delhi since 1947 and the main migration flows", in: Dupont, Veronique; Tarlo, Emma; Vidal, Denis (eds.), *Delhi. Urban Space and Human Destinies*, New Delhi, Manohar/Institut de recherche pour le developppement, 2000; p. 229–52.

Hosagrahar, Jyoti, *Indigenous Modernities. Negotiating Architecture and Urbanism*, New York, Routledge, 2005.

Kalyan, Rohan, *Neo Delhi and the Politics of Postcolonial Urbanism*, London, Routledge, 2021.

Sajjad, Hassan, "Living on the fringes of Delhi—the Ghiyaras of Rangpuri and their continued exclusion", *Minority Rights.org*, 2018, https://minorityrights.org/programmes/library/trends/trends2018/india / (02.02.2023).

Sengupta, Ranjana, *Delhi Metropolitan*, New York, Penguin Books, 2008.

Transport and Communication as Symbols of Modernity in India: A Cultural Perspective

Shraddha Bhatawadekar

Fig. 29: Mumbai, Flora Fountain and the Videsh San-char Bhavam Tower (Tata Communications Limited) in the background.

Postcards constitute an intriguing source for the study of architectural history. Introduced in the late 19th century, picture postcards became popular and continued to be mass produced and used through the Interwar period. Though their heydays could be said to have waned, they still continue to be widely used. Postcards offer enriching glimpses into the transcultural connections of the long 19th century.[1] Technological ad-

---

1   Saloni Mathur has traced the history of postcards in brief and has talked about the role of colonial postcards in relation to India by analysing how gender and

vancements in photography and production aided improvement in their quality. Photographed in one location, produced in some other country, and consumed in the third, postcards travelled long distances. The circulation patterns of the postcards and the study of messages written therein can give valuable insights into the socio-cultural milieu of the time. However, a postcard as a source for the study of architectural history is still less established. For one, they offer static and frozen views of the times when the photograph was taken. Secondly, the settings are often hegemonic, staged to convey particular image and meaning of the architecture. It thus becomes difficult to reconstruct the whole story of architecture from mere postcards.

Nonetheless, they become a visual corollary to archives and other literary sources. Especially, for understanding the history of transport and communication which is more volatile in nature, they form a very useful source. This paper highlights the importance of postcards for the study of architectural history, particularly to understand developments in transport and communication in India, reflecting shifting modernities. The collection available here is a small one, consisting of six postcards:

1. General Post Office, Mumbai
2. Victoria Terminus, Mumbai[2]
3. Western Railway Office, Mumbai
4. Western Railway Offices, Churchgate,[3] Mumbai

---

social representations were manifested through postcards. Mathur, Saloni, *India by Design: Cultural History and Cultural Display*, Berkeley, University of California Press, 2007.

2   Now renamed Chhatrapati Shivaji Maharaj Terminus (2017). For historical references, the name Victoria Terminus is retained, wherever necessary. The photograph in the postcard depicts the administrative headquarters of Central Railway.

3   Two postcards depict western railway offices; one being the headquarter of Western Railway built in 1900 and the office building from the 1950s across the street at Churchgate railway station in Mumbai.

5. Bombay Airport, Mumbai
6. New Telephone Exchange, Kolkata[4]

This collection is rather fragmentary to reconstruct the entire narrative, but it offers an important visual account of different genres in transport and communication architecture in India. Buildings that were built for the purposes of transport and communication, be it for administrative or daily use, were in constant flux. As technologies advanced and the user needs changed, these buildings were altered, expanded; sometimes remodelled or rebuilt; often extensions were built in the same premises or in different locations to cater to the changing demands of the time. A utilitarian infrastructure, these buildings have received less attention in research. Though the scenario is changing,[5] much more remains to be done. In many cases, the history of buildings, their architecture and temporal-spatial transformations are hard to reconstruct for paucity of archival and literary sources and lack of research.

Especially, in cases of buildings constructed after Indian independence, records are often hard to locate. Visual material can come to the aid here, as the postcards in this collection. These postcards are also useful for establishing histories and transformations in institutions; for in-

---

4   The name of the city has now changed from Calcutta to Kolkata (renamed 2001). For historical references, the name Calcutta is retained, wherever necessary.

5   Nitin Sinha has carried out a review of the recent scholarship on transport and communication history of South Asia. As he writes, railway research has expanded into socio-cultural history of railways beyond mere political and financial histories of railway construction. Moreover, "other forms of transport, such as steamships, boats, roadways, and bullock carts" are also being increasingly studied. He adds how communication history is being viewed via "a renewed and distinct focus through the lens of technology, particularly the telegraph…". However, the socio-cultural history of transport-communication architecture remains to be explored. The colonial architecture is well described and assessed in various previous works, but their changing forms and continuities remain yet to be fully explored. Nitin, Sinha, "Histories of transport and communication", *The Journal of Transport History*, Vol. 42(I), 2021; p. 142–69.

stance, the General Post Office building depicted as a sketch in the post-card here was built in the 1870s in Bombay and was subsequently handed over to the Central Telegraph Office in the early 20th century when a new grand building was constructed for the General Post Office at a different location.

Fig. 30: Mumbai, General Post Office, 1913.

Postcards in this collection offer many other useful hints about the socio-cultural histories. While they depict these buildings within the urban setting, as seen in case of the postcard depicting Victoria Terminus, they also celebrate technological advancements, such as the Bombay Airport. Though this paper does not dive deep into the details of the production as well as the messages conveyed through these postcards, preliminary observations show that the postcards were likely circulated in the second half of the 20th century (c. 1970s).[6] The three buildings of this postcard collection, i.e. Victoria Terminus, Western Railway Office, General Post Office were built in the late 19th century. These postcards set these buildings in their mid-20th century context and show how these buildings were adapted/ transformed and used in the 20th century. This

---

6   This is evident from the postal stamps used on the postcards. However, some postcards were never used.

continuity is particularly interesting when viewed within the frame of the use of colonial architecture in the post-colonial times. Throughout this time, the notions of architectural modernism and aesthetics kept shifting. This diachronic approach is less explored in the case of architecture related to infrastructure in India. Using the examples of available postcards as a basis, this paper traces reflections of modernity in transport and communication architecture in India and its role and perceptions in society today.[7]

Transport and Communication as Agents of Modernity

19th century witnessed revolutionary transformations in transport and communication all over the world. The Industrial Revolution provided a great impetus to the development of new technologies, which accelerated progress in transport and communication. The beginning of the railways in 1825[8] following the invention of a steam locomotive dawned a new era in transportation, which not only contributed to enhancing the mobility of people and goods but also had wide repercussions on empire- and nation building. Similarly, innovations in communication

---

7   This paper primarily discusses architectural modernities through the available postcard collection. Thus, the geographical and typological scope of this paper remains limited. Many other forms of transport and communication: roads, ports, etc. are not analysed in this paper. Moreover, post offices, telegraph offices, telephone exchange are integral channels of communication and are only briefly discussed. This postcard collection primarily consists of infrastructures from Bombay and Calcutta. Postcards from Madras (now Chennai) or even other regions of India are absent in the collection and consequently not addressed in the paper. Despite these limitations, this paper highlights the juxtapositions of change and continuity and modernity in transport and communication infrastructure in India.

8   The first railway ran between Stockton and Darlington in 1825. The first fully timetabled railway service—Liverpool and Manchester Railway with freight and passenger traffic opened in 1830. https://www.britannica.com/technology /history-of-technology/Steam-locomotive (07.02.2023).

were spearheaded with the introduction of a telegraph (1837) and telephone (1876), which connected the world in a short span of time.[9] On the one hand, transport and communication led to the 'annihilation of space and time', but on the other, also created new definitions of time and space.[10] They impacted and transformed economic, socio-cultural life of the everyday. Transport and communication systems became harbingers of new modernity in the industrialising and globalising world.

Fig. 31: Mumbai, Victoria Terminus.

These new institutions needed infrastructure for their own operations. The buildings constructed for these purposes resonated architectural trends of the time. Especially headquarters and buildings in important cities were built as monumental structures with elaborate decorations. As Asta von Schroeder writes, "By mid-nineteenth century, the

---

9   https://www.britannica.com/technology/history-of-technology/Steam-locomotive (07.02.2023).

10   Wolfgang Schivelbusch has discussed this concept in detail. Schivelbusch, Wolfgang, "Railroad Space and Railroad Time", *New German Critique*, 1978/14; p. 31–40. https://doi.org/10.2307/488059 (07.02.2023).

railroad was firmly established in the Western World and formed an important part of life in the industrial era. Fighting for a place amongst the league of theatres, museums, and city halls, railway stations took an increasingly representative appearance. The more elaborate contemporary historicist station architecture became, the more often it allowed for extensive decoration programs" (Schroeder 2013: 1). For instance, be it Euston in London, Frankfurt am Main in Germany, Gare de Lyon in Paris, they were all adorned with sculptures that represented modern values and ideas of the time, such as industry, trade, technology, progress.[11] Similarly, telegraph and post offices also acquired a prominent presence on the cityscape; examples included the General Post Office, Central Telegraph Office in London,[12] Central Telegraph Office, Central Post Office in Paris.[13] Such was the prominence of these institutions in the late 19th century that they constituted among the key indicators of modernity.

Colonial Undertones in Transport and Communication in India

The development of transport and communication in India is intrinsically linked with the Colonial Empire. Both transport and communication were essential for the spread as well as control of the Empire. Minutes by Governor General of India Lord Dalhousie in the 1850s highlighted the need for good transportation and communication as a means of economic prosperity as well as military and administrative control (cited in Hurd and Kerr 2012: 9). There was often an underlying notion of progress and civilisation implied in the development of transport

---

11   Asta von Schroeder has carried out a detailed study of iconography of metropolitan railway stations from 1850 to 1950 and the messages they conveyed. Schroeder von, Asta, "Images and Messages in the Embellishment of Metropolitan Railway Stations (1850–1950)", Berlin, Technical University Berlin, 2013.

12   Both structures from the 19th century have been demolished. https://www.post almuseum.org/blog/190-years-of-londons-post-office-quarter/# (07.02.2023).

13   https://archello.com/project/la-poste-du-louvre (07.02.2023).

and communication. At the same time, local traders and influential citizens had also shown interest in these infrastructures. For instance, in Bombay, a group called 'Bombay Great Eastern Railway' was established in the early 1840s by the local elite to promote the cause of railways.[14] Many private British companies also pushed for developing railways in India for the commercial benefits they sought through this enterprise. On 16th April 1853, the first railway ran in Bombay laid by the Great Indian Peninsula Railway Company (hereafter GIPR). The line in Calcutta started in 1854, which was operated by the East Indian Railway Company (hereafter EIR), followed by Madras opened by the Madras Railway Company in 1856. The railways made rapid progress in the next 20 years. By the early 1870s, the major trunk lines were completed connecting the Presidency cities of Bombay, Calcutta and Madras. They came to be used by the British and Indians alike. The railways were an important infrastructure that spurred the growth of metropolises. They became the central landmarks and nodes around which many businesses were aligned. They were well connected to ports and became the gateways to the cities. Railway stations became important markers in public life. The temporary makeshift structures soon gave way to grand modern structures with state-of-the-art facilities for passengers, primarily for first and second classes.

Post offices witnessed early developments from the late 18th century. In 1787, a postmaster was appointed for communication between important towns. It was subsequently followed by the establishment of a General Post Office and the commencement of overseas postal communication before the turn of the century (Chaudhari 1987: 759–760).

---

14   "Classified Ad 5- no Title, *The Bombay Times and Journal of Commerce* (1838–1859), Jul 20, 462, 1844. Later, the group was renewed into an Inland Railway Association in Bombay and merged its interests with the Great Indian Peninsula Railway Company, a private joint-stock company established in England to promote the cause of railways in Bombay and the surrounding region. "Article 2--no Title: Abstract of Accounts of The Great Eastern Railway Company", *The Bombay Times and Journal of Commerce*, Aug 09, 1845; p. 527.

Telegraph was introduced in India 1854 and all main lines were connected between Bombay, Calcutta, and Madras in the next few years (Chaudhari 1987: 761). In the 1860s, India was connected with Europe via telegraph lines. As these networks grew, infrastructure was needed for their operations. Transport and communication infrastructures were well integrated in the urban planning programmes of the late 19th century, mainly in principal cities in India. The architectural styles chosen often corresponded with the architectural styles of other public buildings of the time. In Bombay, acceleration in public building activity took place in the late 1860s following the demolition of Fort that once stood to protect the core settlement from the early 18th century. With the initiative of the then Governor Sir Bartle Frere and planner James Trubshawe, a systematic plan for architectural and urban development was drafted and Victorian Gothic, the style then popular in England, was adopted (Dwivedi and Mehrotra 2001: 95). A series of public buildings, such as the Secretariat, University, High Court, Public Works Department were designed in Victorian Neo Gothic style and built along the Esplanade.[15] Within the same visual plane, General Post Office and Central Telegraph Office were constructed in the 1870s, both also in Neo Gothic style.

Designed by James Trubshawe and Walter Paris, the General Post Office was completed in the early 1870s.[16] A handsome three-storey structure, it had two towers with high-pitched roofs dominating the skyscape (Dwivedi and Mehrotra 2001: 100). In the early 20th century, the post office was moved to a new building next to Victoria Terminus railway station. The new building was constructed to the designs of John Begg, consulting architect to the Government. The principle features of the building were the massive circular dome, inspired by the 17th century local architecture from Bijapur- Gol Gumbaz and the large central hall accom-

---

15   Gothic architecture of the time in Bombay has been discussed by many historians; See, for instance, Davies 1985; Charles, Morris, Tindall et. al., 1986; Lang, Desai and Desai, 1997; London, 2002; Morris, 2005.

16   "The new government buildings on the esplanade: the secretariat the ...", *The Times of India*, 1871, Jun 1.

modating different postal functions.[17] As the Post Office moved out of the premises on the Esplanade, it was taken over by the Central Telegraph Office. Their other building, adjacent to it, designed by Walter Paris in the early 1870s in Neo Gothic style, was connected to the newly acquired building.[18]

Fig. 32: Mumbai, Flora Fountain: a major communication junction in the centre of Fort.

The climax in Neo Gothic style in Bombay can be seen at Victoria Terminus. Built for the headquarters of the GIPR, the building was designed by architect Frederick William Stevens. It was completed in 1888 and became the largest public building in Bombay of the time, together with its adjacent station shed catering to the suburban and long-distance traffic (Mehrotra and Dwivedi 2006: 137).[19] The building was characterised by architectural grandeur, rich decorations and lavish treatment of spaces. Of particular significance was the octagonal dome

---

17   http://www.mmrhcs.org.in/index.php/heritage-information-system/informat
ion-system (07.02.2023).

18   "Quicker telegrams: new Bombay...", *The Times of India*, 1916, Mar 11; p. 9.

19   Mehrotra, Dwivedi, 2006. This book discusses the architecture and construction of Victoria Terminus in detail.

which adorned the building, with a 5'6" statue of progress on top. Frederick William Stevens won great acclaim for his designs and execution of Victoria Terminus and earned many other commissions including the designs for the other railway company headquarters in Bombay, i.e. the Bombay Baroda & Central India Railway (hereafter BB&CI). The BB&CI office (completed 1900), smaller in scale and ornamentation than the GIPR offices, still had a charm of its own (Mehrotra and Dwivedi 2000: 73). With a central circular dome and smaller cupolas, it showed a nice transition towards the Indo-Saracenic style, which became a popular style in the early 20th century Bombay.[20]

Whereas the architecture used for transport and communication reflected the popular and current styles of the time, the railway stations predominantly showcased extravagance. Railways were built by the private companies in the 19th century and the competition for new commissions was particularly fierce across the world. According to Schroeder, "In terms of form, the craving for acceptance by the more established social arbiters explains the confident use of representational codes as embodied by allegoric décor, expensive material, generous handling of space...". (Schroeder 2013: 272).

Railway stations were termed "cathedrals of new humanity" (cited in Richards and MacKenzie 1986: 3). The railways were very important for goods traffic and the subsequent industrial and commercial advancements. The symbols depicted on the building are a testimony to the role the railways played. In India, Victoria Terminus was adorned with allegories representing agriculture, commerce, and industry as well as science and engineering were used at various apex points. The climax was the use of Statue of Progress atop the dome (London 2002: 90–92). On the headquarters of the BB&CI building, an allegory of engineering was represented on the central gable (Mehrotra and Dwivedi 2000: 73). Telegraph and post affairs were controlled by the government from the beginning. The use of statuary was less prominent on the telegraph and

---

20   Indo-Saracenic combined Classical and Gothic models of British architecture with Indian and Islamic motifs. For the detailed discussion on the development of this style in India, see, for instance, Tillotson, 1994.

post office buildings though elaborate architectural arrangements were made to house these infrastructures.

Transport and communication architecture had different connotations. Saloni Mathur states, "Native views of India would often celebrate Britain's architectural achievements in the colony through photographs of sites such as a statue of Queen Victoria in Rawalpindi, a post office in Lucknow, or a railway station in Calcutta. These images of British architecture-of buildings, bridges, gateways, and arches-functioned as symbols of Britain's industrial strength in the colony and underscored ideologies of Western progress in India" (Mathur 2007: 116). Transport and communication were considered key agents of progress and civilisation in the 19th century everywhere in the world as already outlined above. The British bringing progress and civilisation to India through these developments was apparent in discussions on a number of occasions in press and media. For instance, when the railways were inaugurated in Bombay in 1853, this idea echoed in the speeches of the dignitaries. Speaking at the inauguration ceremony of the first railway, Sir William Yardley, the then Chief Justice of Bombay, believed that "a well desired system of Railways, ably and prudently executed, would be the most powerful of all worldly instruments of the advancement and civilization in every respect..."[21] James Berkley, the engineer of the GIPR, who worked on the first railways, added: "It may seem a little thing to those who are familiar with the history of recent days, to open a Railway only twenty (20) miles long, but we have today publicly introduced to this rich and populous nation those two great agents, Steam and Iron... in the form of the most powerful system that modern invention has devised for the extension of Commerce and for the promotion of civilization..."[22] This notion reflected in architecture as well. Civilizing and raising the aesthetic taste of Indians was also often mentioned in speeches and newspapers. Sir Richard Temple, the governor of Bombay, complained in 1881, "The style of many British structures was so erroneous or defective as to exercise a

---

21   *The Bombay Times and Journal of Commerce*. Apr 16, 1855, cited in: Sharma, 1985; p. 17.

22   *Ibid.*

debasing influence on the minds of those Natives, who might be induced to admire or imitate it as being the production of a dominant and presumably a more civilized race" (Evenson 1989: 60). Transport and communication infrastructure served the key purpose to promote the government agenda as they were frequented by local citizens and Europeans alike.

At the same time, they represented the global values promoted in the 19th century as consequences of the industrial Revolution. Multiple similarities can be found in the way this architecture and its use developed and evolved across the world. Innovations in technology and new ways of living were equated with modernity of the time. This urge towards becoming 'modern' was well desired in architecture and urban planning. For instance, when Victoria Terminus was being constructed, the Bombay Government insisted on a modern building that would align with city's image. The Architect of 1886 notes: "Various plans for the new offices and station were submitted to the directors and the Government from time to time, but none of them were approved of, as they failed to satisfy one of the principal conditions laid down, that they should be suited to the importance of the city, and in consonance with its modern architectural features."[23] While these buildings served the representational purposes, they were primarily functional buildings. A lot of attention was given to creating state-of-the-art facilities and comforts. But they also shaped the society by facilitating certain behaviours and realigned the notions of gender, class, and race and had wider economic, socio-cultural impact.

Changing Architectural Norms of the 20th Century

In the early 20th century, the shift in the idea of modernity was apparent and reflected in architecture as well. During this period in India, use of electricity became more common. Technology continued to evolve;

---

23   "An Indian Railway Terminus", The Architect, 1886, Vol. XXXV; p. 15–18.

transport and communication systems got transformed. Railway transport increased multi-fold. Trams were electrified; motor transport was
introduced. Along with telegraph, telephones started being more common in use. As transport and communication infrastructures continued
to penetrate distant regions in India, the existing architecture proved
inadequate to accommodate the rising demands. New buildings had to
be constructed for this purpose. For these constructions, different architectural styles were chosen than their previous counterparts. Among the
most impressive developments in railway architecture in the early 20th
century was the construction of the principal railway station of the EIR
at Howrah. The new station was constructed by demolishing an existing smaller station, originally built in 1854. The Howrah station designed
by Halsey Ricardo, a well-known supporter of arts and crafts movement
(Morris 2005: 128). With its eight towers and symmetrical facades, it was
a masterpiece with Moorish-Romanesque influences. Opened in 1906,
the red-brick station was impressive for its scale; this was the largest station in India and continues to hold this status even today.

Fig. 33: Howrah, New Railway Station.

E.I.R. New Railway Station, Howrah

As traffic increased, need was felt for more infrastructure to suffice
the traffic and technological transformations. In the 1920s and 30s,
both principal stations on GIPR and BB&CI, i.e. Victoria Terminus

and Churchgate were remodeled and new building extensions were erected. Both these buildings were characterized by simplistic style but with modern facilities. Steel-frame and reinforced cement concrete were popular building materials of the time. Nonetheless, they complimented their earlier counterparts in the choice of facing material of stone and layouts. This modern movement in architecture in the 20th century moved away from previous aesthetics. According to Norma Evenson, "The unadorned grandeur of certain industrial structures inspired concepts of a new monumentality, while commercial blocks provided an aesthetic based on the expression of structural framing elements" (Evenson 1989: 158). While technological innovations were at the heart of this modern architecture, elaborate ornamentation of the previous genre was discarded. During this time, transport and communication infrastructures had become integral to public life. The colonial underpinnings of these systems were already overshadowed with their utilitarian nature. It was perhaps also the reason that their transition into the post-independence period was rather smooth.

Utilitarian Needs of the Post-Independence Period

Indian independence in 1947 further accelerated the demand for these infrastructures. They were essential for building new India and the newly established sovereign Government of India advocated the strengthening of these infrastructures for the development and progress of the new nation. As Marian Aguiar argues, "Given the centrality of technological development during the colonial period, it is not surprising that after independence, the railway would maintain its key ideological role within India. The train, previously a symbol of colonial rule, became the sign of an independent, industrialized nation" (Aguiar 2011: 102). Once more, the rising pressure on transport and communication infrastructure necessitated construction of new buildings. During this phase, RCC highrise structures, the common norm of the time, was adopted. These new buildings once again reflected the quest for modernism.

At Churchgate terminus in Bombay, a new station building was erected in 1956, as can be seen in the postcard. As the Maharashtra State Gazetteer outlines, "Due to tremendous expansion of industry and trade in this metropolis, traffic on the suburban section has increased a good deal and old station had to be remodeled" (Chaudhari 1987: 651). Following its construction in the late 19th century, the station underwent changes a number of times. Finally, in the mid-1950s, a seven storeyed building was constructed with a spacious concourse hall, which included all visitor amenities.

Fig. 34: Kolkata, New Telephone Exchange.

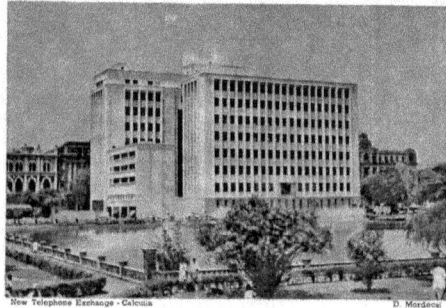

The telephone services also underwent massive expansions during this period. The telephones were inaugurated in Calcutta, Madras, and Bombay in 1882. While the government controlled the telephone lines, it offered licenses to private companies to establish telephone exchanges, with Oriental Telephone Company Limited receiving the initial contract in 1881. The Calcutta Central Exchange was located in 1, Council House Street.[24] The use of telephones picked up manifold

---

24   http://www.calcutta.bsnl.co.in/mainfooter/MainFooter_Company.html#:~:te xt=28th%20January%2C%201882%20is%20a,in%20Calcutta%2C%20Madra s%20and%20Bombay (07.02.2023).

in the post-independence period.[25] As demands rose, a new Telephone Exchange building was erected at Dalhousie Square (now BDD Bagh) in the mid-1950s. Not much information could be gathered about the New Telephone Exchange. This seven storey structure seems to have been erected by the firm of Ballardie, Thompson, and Matthews in 1956.[26] Known as Telephone Bhavan, it enjoyed a vantage position in central Calcutta together with several other systems, including General Post Office and Telegraph Office. Along with roads and railways, a new form of transport was popularised in the post-independence period. The air transport was slow to develop in India. Despite early efforts in the beginning of the 20th century, the air traffic remained limited. The Civil Aviation Department constituted in 1927 and aerodromes were created. A few air services were introduced, such as Imperial Airways Service running between Croydon and Delhi and the service introduced by the Tata Airways Ltd. in 1932 within the Indian subcontinent (Chaudhari 1987: 657–58). However, it was only after independence that the service was expanded. The construction of Bombay Airport on the location of previous Air Force hangers at Santacruz began in the early 1950s and the new airport was opened for traffic in 1958 to handle the increasing domestic and international passenger traffic.[27] The terminal building consisted of modern facilities for passenger conveniences. Within the next two decades, a new terminal at Sahar was added to cater to the increasing international services. As public infrastructure, the transport and communication systems continued to be expanded. They were already localised but were further appropriated through name changes. In the 1950s, the railway system was reorganised and the GIPR became Central Railway and BB&CI was incorporated into Western Railway;

25   It was taken over by the Post and Telegraph Department of the Government of India in 1943. In 1985, the post and telegraph were separated, and telephone came under the Department of Telecom. In 2000, Bharat Sanchar Nigam Limited (BSNL) was established as a central public sector undertaking.

26   http://wikimapia.org/174005/Telephone-Bhavan (07.02.2023).

27   "Construction of New Buildings: BOMBAY AIRPORT", The Times of India, May 4, 1957; p.2. The new terminal for international traffic was opened at Sahar in the vicinity of the Santacruz airport in 1980. Chaudhari, 1987; p. 659–60.

EIR was reconstituted as Eastern Railway; all as branches of Indian Railways, a public entity. Subsequently, the names of stations also changed so also of the principal cities. Victoria Terminus became Chhatrapati Shivaji Terminus in 1996, (later renamed Chhatrapati Shivaji Maharaj Terminus in 2017).[28] Bombay Airport also assumed the name of Chhatrapati Shivaji International Airport in 1999 (later renamed Chhatrapati Shivaji Maharaj International Airport in 2018).[29] Public memory has still retained the old names to a great extent. It offers testimony to affinities people have developed over time with these systems. They are integral to the functioning of everyday and have become the lifelines for people. They are also landmarks in the regions they serve, but their importance transcends beyond as cultural icons of the country.

Fig. 35: Mumbai, Western Railway Office.

---

28   "Mumbai's Chhatrapati Shivaji Terminus renamed to Chhatrapati Shivaji Maharaj Terminus", *India Today*, Jun 30, 2017. https://www.indiatoday.in/educa tion-today/gk-current-affairs/story/mumbai-chhatrapati-shivajiterminus-ren amed-1021708-2017-06-30 (07.02.2023).

29   "Mumbai airport renamed as Chhatrapati Shivaji 'Maharaj' International Airport.", *The Indian Express*, Aug 30., 2018. https://indianexpress.com/article/in dia/mumbai-airport-chhatrapati-shivaji-maharaj-international-airport-53332 52/ (07.02.2023).

Transport and Communication as Heritage Symbols

Many of the transport and communication infrastructures from the 19th and 20th century continue to be in use even today. Given their architectural aesthetics and historical importance, these structures have become heritage landmarks. In Mumbai, a heritage list was created by the Brihanmumbai Municipal Corporation in 1995, in which properties have been graded as I, IIA & B and III (Heritage Regulations for Greater Bombay 1995). While Central Telegraph Office is Grade IIA, both Chhatrapati Shivaji Maharaj Terminus and Western Railway Offices are Grade I structures. In addition, Victoria Terminus has been inscribed on a UNESCO World Heritage List since 2004, which has elevated its status internationally (CST Nomination File 945rev 2004). However, what the heritage designation often overlooks is the continued use and technological and industrial values that these monuments possess.

If one looks at the existing transport and communication infrastructure today, one can often find traces of original structures, built in the early 19th and 20th century. They have been expanded, refurbished with changing technologies, and needs of space, time, and societies. The use of new materials, technological innovations, constant experimentations, and evolutions have characterised these infrastructures. This technological and industrial aesthetics is also an integral part of their heritage, hitherto less explored. Change is constant in case of infrastructures, but one can see continuities in these systems as well. This functionality of heritage should be taken into account and other ancillary built and intangible elements that embody this heritage should be identified. This postcard collection with its focus on highlighting the transport and communication infrastructures aims to bring about awareness of their values and expand the notions of their heritage. They have been previously looked at as parts of urban or architectural history, but their role as infrastructures and their relations to the everyday functioning or as emblems of technology and shifting modernity opens up new perspectives of looking at them not just as isolated structures but within their changing contexts. In this case, heritage also assumes the function of managing change to ensure their future sustenance while retaining their historical, aesthetic, and cultural importance.

References

Aguiar, Marian, *Tracking Modernity: India's Railway and The Culture of Mobility*, Minneapolis, University of Minnesota Press, 2011.

Allen, Charles; Morris, Jan; Tindall, Gillian; Amery, Colin; Stamp, Gavin, *Architecture of the British Empire*, London, Weidenfeld and Nicolson, 1986.

Chaudhari, K. K., *Maharashtra State Gazetteers: Greater Bombay District*, Vol. II., 1987.

CST Nomination File 945rev 2004. http://whc.unesco.org/en/list/945.

Davies, Philip, *Splendours of the Raj: British Architecture in India, 1660 to 1947*, London, John Murray, 1985.

Dwivedi, Sharada; Mehrotra, Rahul, *Bombay: The Cities Within*, Mumbai, Eminence, 2001.

Evenson, Norma, *The Indian Metropolis: A View Toward the West*, New Haven, Yale University Press, 1989.

Heritage Regulations for Greater Bombay, Urban Development Department, Government of Maharashtra. Mumbai 1995, revised 2012.

Hurd, John; Kerr, Ian J., *India's Railway History- A Research Handbook*, Leiden, BRILL, 2012.

Lang, Jon; Desai, Madhavi; Desai, Miki, *Architecture and Independence: The Search for Identity—India 1880 to 1980*, London, Oxford University Press, 1997.

London, Christopher W., *Bombay Gothic*, Mumbai, India Book House, 2002.

Mehrotra, Rahul; Dwivedi, Sharada, *Anchoring a City Line 1899–1999: The history of the western suburban railway and its headquarters in Bombay*, Mumbai, Eminence, 2000.

Mehrotra, Rahul, *A City Icon: Victoria Terminus, Bombay 1887; Now Chhatrapati Shivaji Terminus, Mumbai 1996*, Mumbai, Eminence, 2006.

Mann, Michael, "The Deep Digital Divide: The Telephone in British India 1883–1933", in: *Historical Social Research / Historische Sozialforschung* 35/1, 2010; p. 188–208, http://www.jstor.org/stable/20762435

Morris, Jan, *Stones of Empire: The Buildings of the Raj*, New York, Oxford University Press, first published 1983; 2005.

Richards, Jeffrey; MacKenzie, John M., *The Railway Station: A Social History*, Oxford, Oxford University Press, 1986.

Sharma, S. N., *History of The Great Indian Peninsula Railway (1853–1869)*, Mumbai, S.D.G.M. Central Railway, 1985.

Tillotson, Giles H. R., "Orientalizing the Raj: Indo-Saracenic Fantasies.", in: *Architecture in Victorian and Edwardian India*, Mumbai, Marg Publications, 1994; p. 15–34.

Before take-off: waiting for India's globalization at the Sahar International Airport in 1974

Yves-Marie Rault-Chodankar

Fig. 36/37: Left: Mumbai, Sahar International Airport, photograph from the 1960s. Right: Verso of the above-mentioned postcard.

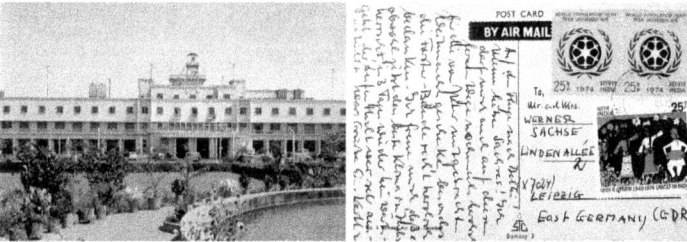

"On my way to Delhi! My dear Sachse! Let me thank you one more time for the Christmas gifts Nehr got me, especially Forster's volumes. I am glad he'll go back in three days, even though India's climate is now at its best, but the stay was hectic. 1000 greetings from [unreadable name]"

These few lines by a German traveler, written to a friend in Leipzig, suggest that the purpose of his Indian trip was not tourism. His journey was hectic, and he is happy that his friend can return to Germany, even though, as he notes, the weather has turned pleasant. Looking at the postage stamps, we can guess that it is early or late 1974 in Mumbai when the city enjoys the moderate sun of winter. Not a tourist, he probably is not a hippy either. In the 1970s, the many Westerners who traveled to India to experience the local spiritual heritage did it through the "hippie trail," a popular overland route that went through countries such as Turkey, Iran, Afghanistan, Pakistan, and finally, India. But our German traveler picked a photo of Mumbai's airport, suggesting he was travelling by air, a true privilege in the 1970s when a round-trip from Germany to India could have cost the price of a car.

The Sahar International Airport, as it was then named, is photographed from its outside. The photograph captures the terminal's entrance, with its pristine white concrete walls supported by light pillars. The flowers add a touch of warmth and beauty to the scene, creating a striking contrast with the concrete and steel of the airport. The red flowers of the West Indian Jasmine, widely used in weddings, bloom throughout the year in South Asia. As for the sunflowers, a symbol of hope and renewal, they seem to be a fitting metaphor for the airport that was going to take India on a global journey.

When India was sleeping: the modest role of Mumbai airport in 1970s India

However, in the early 1970s, India was still sleeping. In the photograph, the airport is deserted, and the only movement in the picture comes from the parked cars, which gives a sense of stillness and emptiness. The Sahar International Airport was built during the British colonial period in India. It was commissioned by the British government and constructed by the Public Works Department of the British Government in India. After India's independence, the airport was nationalized and was placed under the control of the Indian government, managed by the Ministry of Civil Aviation and later by the Airports Authority of India, which is responsible for developing and managing airports in India. As a functional building, mostly meant to fulfill the needs of the colonial administration, the airport was the opposite of impressive. What strikes is the minimalism of the façade of the terminal building, in the epoch of Art Deco. In addition to the main terminal building, the airport also had several other buildings and facilities built in the same architectural style, such as the control tower, the cargo terminal, and the maintenance hangars.[1] When it would be revamped as the modern Chhatrapati Shivaji International Airport in the 21st century, the airport would over-emphasize Indian elements such as dome-shaped roofs, arches, tall and slender columns with traditional Indian motifs. In the early 1970s, the Sahar International Airport could not accommodate more than 600 passengers at any time and served a limited number of domestic and international destinations.[2] Also, it hosted a few cargo flights, transporting sensitive goods such as electronic components, machinery, and high-value goods. The postcard was probably sent by airmail service, along with other small packages and parcels.

Dreaming of greatness: the ambitions of an Indian airport

Still, the Sahar International Airport was India's largest airport at the time, and the main entry gate to the country, probably explaining why our German traveler first landed in Mumbai. The cities of Delhi, Kolkata, Chennai, Ahmedabad, Bengaluru, and Hyderabad also had international airports, but Mumbai was a major center of cotton trade and textile production and the main financial hub of India, connected to the world.[3] Also, it was home to the famous Tata Airlines. The airline is

---

1   For a view of the airport in 1970, see Mumbai Airport, 1970s India, HD from 16mm, YouTube. s. d. URL: https://www.youtube.com/watch?v=oQDGa7g_P_I &ab_channel=Kinolibrary (15.02.2023).

2   Shoba, Gupta; Singh, Uday Chander, "Travellers Can Breathe Freely with Brand New and Improved Terminal at Sahar in Bombay", *India Today*, 31/12/1980. URL: https://www.indiatoday.in/magazine/tourism/story/19801231-travellers-can-b reathe-freely-with-brand-new-and-improved-terminal-at-sahar-in-bombay-7 73676-2013-11-29 (15.02.2023).

3   Patel, S.; Masselos, J. (eds.), *Bombay and Mumbai: The City in Transition*, New Delhi, New York, Oxford University Press, 2003.

intertwined with the history of India's aviation.[4] It was founded in 1932 as Tata Airlines, later nationalized in 1946 and renamed Air India. In the 1950s, Air India became one of the first carrier in the world to operate jet aircraft, and it was also one of the first airlines to fly to the United States and Canada. When Sahar International Airport was built and opened in 1942, the company was one of the main carriers operating out of the airport, alongside Indian Airlines, which mainly served domestic routes. Amongst the foreign airlines, the leading ones were British Airways, Air France, Lufthansa, KLM, and Pan American Airways. Although the airport looks asleep in the photograph, India was on the cusp of a significant transformation. A symbol of British colonial engineering, it became the symbol of India's dream of greatness as India gained its independence in 1947. In the early 1970s, the country was emerging from its post-independence economic struggles and was starting to industrialize, leaving behind its primarily agricultural economy.[5] The development and operation of a major international airport like Sahar International Airport represented a significant investment in the country's transportation infrastructure. It symbolized the country's will to integrate with the global economy and its efforts to project a modern and progressive image of India.

Rooting for the world: locating the airport in Mumbai

The airport's location, near the city of Mumbai, made it easily accessible to the large population of the city, and it was also located near the coast, which allowed for aircraft to take off and land over the sea, reducing the noise pollution over the residential areas. Located in the suburb of Santa Cruz, it was built on land primarily used for agriculture and was relatively flat and open, making it ideal for constructing runways

---

4   Tata J., "The Sixteenth British Commonwealth Lecture: The Story of Indian Air Transport", *Current Science*, 1994; p. 455–479.

5   Rothermund, Dietmar, *India: The rise of an Asian giant*, Yale, Yale University Press, 2008.

and taxiways. In the 1970s, it would have taken 45 minutes to an hour to reach Colaba by taxi, as the airport was not well connected to public transportation. It was however signaling an early shift in the city-core of Mumbai.[6]

Our German traveler, as he left the airport, would have first passed through the surrounding neighborhoods, likely a mix of small, densely populated residential and commercial areas with small shops and businesses.[7] The buildings in these areas would probably be relatively low-rise, made of brick or concrete. He would then likely see more open spaces and greenery, including small farms and fields, wetlands, and mangrove forests.

Fig. 38: North-western suburb of Mumbai, residential buildings built in the 1970s.

These areas would be dotted with small villages and rural communities with traditional occupations such as fishing. Getting closer to Co-

---

6   Sita, K.; Phadke, V.S.; Swapna, Banerjee (eds.), *The Declining City-Core of an Indian Metropolis: A Case Study of Bombay*, New Delhi, Concept Pub. Co., 1988.

7   For photos of Mumbai during its transformative years after independence till the early 1990s, see: Dwivedi, Sharada; Mehrotra Rahul, *Bombay The Cities within*, Mumbai, Eminence, 2001.

laba, our traveler would start to see more densely populated areas, with taller buildings and more developed infrastructure. The streets would be more crowded, and there would be more traffic. Alongside establishments from the Victorian period, he could begin to see a few buildings made of concrete and glass.

Rising above the Paddy: the transformation of Mumbai's airport

The airport's area of Santa Cruz, once in the suburbs of Mumbai, is now at the heart of the city. From a population of about 6 million inhabitants in the 1970s, the city hosted more than 21 million individuals in 2023, transforming the face of the city.[8] Thanks to its easy access to international and domestic travel, Santa Cruz has accommodated several large companies, including multinational corporations, which has led to the development of many service-based industries, such as banking, finance, and insurance.[9] The transformation of the airport, known as Chhatrapati Shivaji Maharaj International Airport since 1999, reflects the growing demand for air travel in Mumbai and India.

As India liberalized and globalized in the 1980s, putting an end to the "Hindu" rate of growth (a witty term invented for the 3.5% rate of growth that had prevailed till then), the airport underwent several expansions and renovations to keep up with the growing demand for air travel. With the liberalization of India's economy in the 1990s, the airport expanded to accommodate larger aircraft and to improve passenger facilities. In 2006, like most Indian airports, it was privatized and bought

---

8   Saglio, Marie-Caroline, "Mumbai: mutations spatiales d'une métropole en expansion", *Mappemonde* 62/2, 2001; p.26-31. URL: https://doi.org/10.3406/mappe.2001.1654 (15.02.2023).

9   Imbach, Ruedi, "Vers une «global city region»? Stratégies économiques, déploiement spatial et politiques d'accompagnement à Mumbai", *Métropoles*, 2011/9. URL: https://metropoles.revues.org/4469 (15.02.2023).

by the Adani group, owned by one of the country's wealthiest men, a ty-coon whose fortune was made by developing global infrastructures in India. The old terminal, visible in the photo, does not exist anymore and has been replaced by two new terminals. The main terminal building was also stretched and renovated to provide more passenger space, and new facilities, such as duty-free shops and restaurants, were added. With the continuous addition of new runways and taxiways, the airport is now one of the busiest in India. It handles about 50 million passengers and 1 million metric tons of cargo annually.[10]

Our German traveler would not recognize Mumbai's airport any-more. Now a blend of traditional Indian and modern styles, featuring a central dome structure with arched openings and intricate carvings combined with clean lines and sleek glass facades, the airport that once reflected the country's sleepiness now represents the airport's emphasis on global lifestyle and economic prosperity. The India that was waiting at the terminal of the Sahar International Airport in 1974 has taken off.

References

Dwivedi, Sharahdha; Mehrotra, Rahul, *Bombay: The Cities Within*, Mum-bai, Eminence, 2001.

Gupta, Shoba; Singh, Uday Chander, *"Travellers Can Breathe Freely with Brand New and Improved Terminal at Sahar in Bombay,"* India Today, 31 December 1980.

Imbach, Romain, "Vers une 'global city region'? Stratégies économiques, déploiement spatial et politiques d'accompagnement à Mumbai," *Métropoles*, 2011/9.

Patel, Sujata; Masselos, Jim (eds.), *Bombay and Mumbai: The City in Transi-tion*, New Delhi& New York, Oxford University Press, 2003.

Rothermund, Dieter, *India: The rise of an Asian giant*, New Haven, Yale Uni-versity Press, 2008.

---

10   "About us | Mumbai International Airport (BOM) | CSMIA", URL: https://csmia .adaniairports.com/about-us.aspx (15.02.2023).

Saglio, Marie-Caroline, "Mumbai: mutations spatiales d'une métropole en expansion," *Mappemonde* 62, 2001/2; p. 26–31.

Sita, K.; Phadke, V. S.; Swapna, Banerjee, *The Declining City-Core of an Indian Metropolis: A Case Study of Bombay*, New Delhi, Concept Pub. Co, 1988.

Tata, Dadabhoy R. Jehangir, "The Sixteenth British Commonwealth Lecture: The Story of Indian Air Transport," *Current Science*, 1994; p. 455–79.

Fig. 39: Mumbai, Malabar Point and Bombay Bay in 1900, before the international economic boom and trade globalization.

The Taj Mahal Hotel, Imperial, Sun'n'Sand, Oberoi, and others: the Indian chapter of the 20th-century grand hotel

Éléonore Muhidine

Fig. 40: *New Delhi, Interior courtyard of the Oberoi Hotel in the 1970s.*

The postcards showing views of luxury hotels, most of them 5-star rated, located in the cities of Mumbai, New Delhi, and Agra, are perhaps the least critical visual resources of the collection. As advertising objects, products of the mass tourism industry, these images seek only to seduce their recipient—and potential future client—with the sweet promise of an unforgettable stay. Whether shot from the front or at an angle, the images of these grand hotels give an impression of fortress architecture, impregnable modern and generic monuments that seem to guarantee an untroubled holiday, their luxurious rooms, gourmet restaurants, and relaxation areas sealed off from the outside world. On the reverse of the cards, the desire to seduce continues: "luxurious living" "Fully air-conditioned," "Finest cuisine", "Swimming Pool," "Symbol of Luxury, Comfort and Good Living," "Overlooking the Taj Mahal." The hotels have been locations for international film productions[1] – and, in the case of the Taj Mahal and Oberoi Trident hotels, sites of terrorist incidents (in 1993 and 2008). Beyond the dramatic topography and associations with events that temporarily damaged their public image, these large hotels, built between 1902 and 1973, reflect the political and economic transformation of India in the 20th century: the ardent desire for independence embodied by the Swadeshi movement; the rise of corporations such as the steel giant Tata; and foreign covetousness towards a region of huge potential.

The grand hotels of India: urban markers of decolonization and Independence (Taj Mahal Hotel, Ashok, Oberoi, and Clarks)

An Indian project par excellence, the Taj Mahal Hotel (1903) was commissioned by the founder of the Tata group and businessman Jamshedji Tata (1839–1904) and designed by the architect Sitaram Khanderao Vaidya. Born out of one man's ambition to establish Bombay as an international financial centre, India's first grand hotel also represented a reaction against the spatial discrimination that existed around 1900 in Bombay. The city's major hotels had a discriminatory access policy that prohibited Indians from entering. Watson's Hotel and the Apollo, meccas of international cultural sociability in Bombay, were two such. As the architect Rahul Mehrotra observes: "The expansion of the city in the 1890s had led to the construction of more hotels such as the Apollo on Colaba Causeway, but most of these were open only to Europeans. It

---

1   The Taj Mahal Hotel in Mumbai appears in several scenes in Christopher Nolan's film *Tenet* (2020).

was perhaps to counter the racial prejudice of the time that Jamshedji Tata took the decision to build the Taj, where Indians of all castes and creeds could freely socialise amongst themselves and with European on neutral ground."[2] The sense of injustice felt by the limited access policy (we should emphasise the importance of closed social spaces in Bombay, and in particular the many members-only clubs) intensified in the period 1900–1920, when the hotels became cultural spaces with their own events, including jazz concerts[3] and movie screenings. Indeed, in 1896, Watson's Hotel (the first prefabricated steel structure in India, manufactured entirely in England and shipped to Bombay) presented the Lumière brothers' first films.[4] Thus, the grand hotels accelerated the process by which contemporary foreign culture—mainly European and North American—was introduced to India.

The Taj Mahal Hotel, with its neo-historical national architecture – a blend of Gothic inspiration and the traditional style of the Mughal palaces of Rajasthan – is one of the most widely reproduced motifs on postcards of Mumbai. Its location, a few metres from the most representative monument of the capital of Maharashtra, the Gateway of India (a triumphal arch separating the city from the sea), has helped it to become a national and international icon. Another card in the collection shows a model of the Taj Mahal Hotel and its contemporary counterpart, the Taj Mahal Tower, a 22-storey reinforced concrete building designed by the American architect Melton Bekker and the Swiss designer Dale Keller and completed in 1972. Its verticality mirrors that of the hotel. However, while the latter ushered in a new era of luxury palaces run by the local elite, the Tower was a different kind of milestone because it initiated a trend for building high-rises on the waterfront. This was followed by the construction of buildings on Nariman Point (a few hundred metres from

2   Mehrotra, Rahul; Dwivedi, Sharada, *Bombay. The Cities Within*, Eminence, Mumbai, 1995; p. 210.

3   Fernandes, Naresh, *Taj Mahal Foxtrot: The Story of Bombay's Jazz Age*, Mumbai, Roli Books, 2017.

4   Préval de, Jitka, *Camille Legrand. Opérateur Pathé sur la Route des Indes*, Paris, Riveneuve, 2022.

Apollo Bandar Boulevard, the site of the Taj Mahal), most notably the Air India building (1974, architect John Burgee) and the Trident Hotel (1973, architect P. G. Patki).

Fig. 41: New Delhi, Ashok Hotel (1956).

Following India's Independence, Prime Minister Nehru commissioned the architect E. B. Doctor to design the Ashok Hotel in New Delhi for the purpose of accommodating the members of the 9th UNESCO conference (1956). This was a common occurrence in the history of large hotels in India: they were hotspots of international political life, places where Indian and Western leaders congregated to make momentous decisions. For example, in 1946, the Imperial Hotel in New Delhi (1936) hosted a meeting in which Nehru, Gandhi, and Mohammad Ali Jinnah negotiated the partition of India and the creation of the state of Pakistan. The table around which they sat is on display in the hotel.

The Sun'n'Sand (1962) is located in the north-western suburbs of Mumbai. It is representative both of the rise of mass tourism after 1945 and the growth of the greater Bombay suburbs. Located on the waterfront, within easy reach of the international airport, the hotel maintains, in a certain sense, the local tradition of temporary waterfront accommodation (of which the Bombay Sailor's Home [1869] was a prime example).

Fig. 42: Mumbai, The Sun'n'Sand Hotel in the 1960s.

The sponsor of Mumbai's second 5-star hotel (the first being the Taj Mahal Hotel), the Indian entrepreneur Gul Advani, probably had in mind the idea of offering wealthy foreign travellers and the local elites (especially those from the affluent suburb of Bandra-West) a suitable place to relax by the sea and stage large wedding parties (which were, and are, a fundamental feature of Indian life).

The postcard showing the Oberoi Intercontinental in New Delhi (1973) is a testimony to the growth of the eponymous company (est. 1934). The first of Oberoi's many Indian hotels was the Kolkata, which was built on the site of an old theatre that burnt down in 1911, and the first building in Calcutta to be equipped with a hydraulic lift. Originally owned by an Armenian, the hotel was bought by Oberoi sometime in the 1930s. It became infamous when six people died in 1937 from typhoid fever, contracted via the hotel's pipes. The episode marked the sudden (literal) intrusion of India's unsanitary water drainage system into a space that was presented as cut off from the outside world, especially the everyday problems of Indian society. The hotel was rehabilitated and reopened in 1939 as a war hospital for British soldiers. (Many of the European and Indian hotels were requisitioned and put to various uses during the Second World War.)

Fig. 43: New Delhi, Oberoi Intercontinental Hotel.

A brochure of the Oberoi Intercontinental distributed at its opening promised an unprecedented experience of technical modernity:
"Planned with painstaking care and decorated luxuriously, the hotel is
designed to provide the ultimate in comfort and entertainment. Eleven
storeys high, the hotel commands one of the most breath-taking views
of the capital city and overlooks the Delhi Golf course and Humayun's
Tomb. Seven imaginatively planned restaurants offer food for every
taste and budget in a cosmopolitan atmosphere so much a part of all
Oberoi hotels. A modern health club and swimming-pool, a shopping
centre and a great variety of entertainment facilities make Oberoi
Intercontinental the outstanding new venue for all Delhi residents."

Foreign interests: from the New Delhi Imperial to the Bombay Hilton (1936–1960s)

India, which was occupied by several colonial powers at the beginning of the 20th century, did not completely free itself from foreign control after 1947. Economic globalization and the desire for conquest that it engenders are partly responsible. The grand hotels reflected this reality. Some of the buildings depicted on the postcards offer their visitors an interpretation of the nation's past and local heritage, and the boundaries between hotel space and museum space are deliberately blurred.

Fig. 44: New Delhi, Hotel Imperial (1936), Pre-Independence postcard.

The Imperial Hotel (architect F. B. Blomfield), which opened its doors in 1936, is a melting pot of references to British culture and traditional colonialist imaginings of India. Although the publicity leaflets of the time promised the then-fashionable Art Deco style, this could be found only on the façade, which had the aspect of the larger New York hotels, especially the New Yorker (1929). In the numerous interior salons and courtyards, a neo-classical aesthetic inspired by ancient monuments was evident, with numerous colonnades and water basins decorated with Romanesque fountains. Far from breaking with the surrounding city, the hotel was in keeping with the vision of Edwin Lutyens (1869–1944), New Delhi's chief architect.

Fig. 45: A 19th century hotel in old Delhi.[5]

To this day, the Imperial offers its residents a journey across cultures; the "silver tea service, tableware from London, Italian marble floors, Burma teak furniture, original Daniels and Frasers on the walls, a vision of undulating green lawns, turbaned waiters in red, all create

---

5   On the reverse side of the card is handwritten (in German): "hotel according to a European model". Our research did not lead us to find this building, probably destroyed today. However, it is quite similar to some of the buildings in the central avenue of Chandni Chowk.

the aura of an early 19th century English manor in the heart of Imperial Delhi."[6]

It provides a superior experience than its rivals, with a private museum consisting of three art galleries, one dedicated to Indian landscape painting, another based on the theme of "North Indians" (and whose representations of the colonial era should be analysed), and a third comprising paintings, lithographs, and watercolours from the 17th and 18th centuries by British artists in India.

Other major hotel groups blurred the boundary between grand hotel and museum in their bid to conquer the global tourism market, for example, the Hilton Hotel in Cairo (1955). The architectural historian Annabel Jane Wharton describes it thus in *Building the Cold War: Hilton International Hotels and Modern Architecture*:

"The interior decoration maintained the pharaonic theme. The broad entrance lobby had reception on one side and a massive reproduction of a stone relief from the Egyptian Museum on the other: a colossal pharaoh hunting the wildlife of the Nile. In the guest rooms the brass lamp stands were inspired by the lotus and the draperies were hand-blocked with a stylized version of the same flowers [...] In the elite shops of the lobby mall, ancient artifacts and their reproductions were available for purchase, the ultimate form of touristic consumption."[7]

From India to Egypt, the 20th-century grand hotel was a space for the elaboration and dissemination of a discourse on a nation's culture and its past, a discourse dominated by foreign designers inspired by collections of looted objects. Conrad Hilton played a major role in defining the aesthetics of the international grand hotel after 1945 and in propagating an international style theorised as early as 1932 by American authors.

"The Istanbul Hilton [1955] was a heroically scaled white slab constructed of reinforced concrete, scaled by a regular grid of balconies

---

6   From: https://theimperialindia.com/imperial_history/ (12.01.2023).

7   Wharton, Jane Annabel, *Building the Cold War: Hilton International Hotels and Modern Architecture*, Chicago, University of Chicago Press, 2004; p. 50.

and lifted off the ground by slender white pilotis, or piers. Descriptions of the Istanbul Hilton tend to emphasize its similarities to the buildings of Le Corbusier. [...] The new Hilton was a monumental structure enshrined as an elite art object by its exceptional site. The hotel was prestigiously located, positioned at the edge of the wealthiest part of Istanbul, high above Galata. [...] The interior order of the Istanbul Hilton, analogous to its exterior, looked like a photograph from the handbook of American Modernism, Hitchcock, and Johnson's *The International Style.*"[8]

Less well-known is the Hilton hotel project that was planned for Bombay in the early 1960s; it never went past the planning stage because the site lacked the most basic sanitation. In *Bombay imagined*, Robert Stephens describes the scene: "At first glance, the Worli Sea Face appeared to be the perfect location for Hilton's flagship hotel in Bombay. [...] More than 400 luxury rooms were organized in an elongated structure wrapped in a façade of sunshades; a feature Kadria would perfect a decade later while designing the Nehru Centre. A series of low-slung, open-air pavilions at the ground floor framed views of the Arabian Sea and were ideally suited for banquets, evening drinks, or a lazy day by the pool. Hilton's dream soon turned into a nightmare when visiting foreign executives discovered a dirty little secret: the waters of Worli were flushed with raw sewage. Visions of guests lying asphyxiated under seaside pavilions, the unsuspecting victims of Bombay's effluvia, likely provoked many sleepless nights, and the project was dumped soon thereafter."[9]

The Indian grand hotels shared certain architectural (and historical) characteristics. For instance, they were all built in extraordinary locations (either by the sea or with an unobstructed view of one or more historical monuments) and they provided unique facilities (at least for India). Indeed, they endeavoured to give their guests such an experience that they would feel no desire (or need) to venture beyond. However,

---

8   *Ibid.*; p. 22.
9   Stephens, Robert, *Bombay Imagined. An Illustrated History of the Unbuilt City*, Mumbai, Urbsindis, 2022; p. 234–35.

albeit the hotels were cultural spaces with codes and regulations, they were also part of a tradition of similar institutions that began in the capitals of Europe (e.g., Lutetia in Paris, the Bauer in Berlin, and the Bristol in Bucharest) and its seaside resorts (e.g., the Gallia Palace in Cannes, the Hermitage in La Baule, the Riviera in Nice, and the Grand Hotel in Cabourg) and which experienced a boom during the Industrial Revolution. The fashion for grand hotels then spread throughout the world. The Pera district of Istanbul alone saw the construction of the Grand Hotel Kroecker, the Pera Palas Oteli, the Grand Hotel de Londres, and the Grand Hotel Novotny. In each of them, the foreign presence was very marked, not only amongst the guests but also the management.

Fig. 46: Mumbai, View of Marine Drive in the 1970s with the Trident Hotel on Narima Point in the background (1973).

The postcards in question, which in some cases illustrate otherwise concealed spaces and reveal the photographers' predilection for indoor swimming pools, reflect a Western way of life far removed from that of the average Indian. They are also a testament to the post-1945 modernist standardisation of contemporary architectural forms, as exemplified by the master himself, Le Corbusier. Although there is no critical intent behind these images – their purpose is simply to advertise a product – they are nonetheless an important archival source for the modern architectural history of India and, more generally, the history of the 20th century. As such, they merit further scholarly attention.

References

Denby, Elaine, *Grand Hotels: Reality and Illusion*, London, Reaktion Books, 2002.

Fernandez, Naresh, *Taj Mahal Fox Trot. The Story of Bombay's Jazz Age*, New Delhi, Roli Books, 2017.

Mehrotra, Rahul; Dwivedi, Sharada, *Bombay: The Cities Within*, Mumbai, Eminence, 2001.

Préval de, Jitka, *Camille Legrand. Un opérateur Pathé sur la route des Indes 1895–1920*, Paris, Riveneuve, 2021.

Robert, Stephens, *Bombay Imagined. An Illustrated History of the Unbuilt City*, Mumbai, Urbsindis, 2022

Warren, William, *Asia's Legendary Hotels. The Romance of travel*, Singapore, Periplus Editions, 2007.

Wharton, Annabel Jane, *Building the Cold War: Hilton International Hotels and Modern Architecture*, Chicago, University of Chicago Press, 2004.

Image, recto, verso, context. Approaching Deltiology as a method

Ben Kaden

Postcards, as an early and very "viral" form of social media, captivate for many reasons.[1] Their persistent appeal could stem from a peculiar configuration: an intendedly ephemeral short message medium,[2] mass-produced for narrowly defined communicational purposes turns when used into a unique multimodal[3] carrier of social traces, history, stories, i.e. social text. Not least, collecting postcards is an easy and wholesome hobby. In contrast, the research practice known as *delitology* achieved only scattered scholarly attraction so far.[4] The term "deltiology", which some collectors considered to be rather snobbish, arguably traces back

---

1 Pyne, Lydia, *Postcards: The Rise and Fall of the World's First Social Network*, London, Reaktion Books, 2021.

2 Gillen, Julia, "Writing Edwardian postcards", *Journal of Sociolinguistics*, 2013/17; p. 488–521. DOI: 10.1111/josl.12045.

3 Gugganig, Mascha; Schor, Sophie, "Multimodal Ethnography in/of/as Postcards", *American Anthropologist*, 122/3, 2020; p. 691–697. DOI: 10.1111/aman.13435; Gillen, *op.cit.*; Kaden, Ben, "My Dear Mother" Multimodalität als Herausforderung bei der Auseinandersetzung mit Ansichtskarten, *retraceblog*, 01.11.2021, https://retraceblog.wordpress.com/2021/11/01/my-dear-mother-multimodalitat-als-herausforderung-bei-der-auseinandersetzung-mit-ansichtskarten/ (02.03.2023); Pyne, *op.cit.*

4 As of February, Google Scholar has just about 240 articles that somehow mention "deltiology". The somehow related field of "Philately" lists about 12600. However, "deltiology" itself is a niche term. There are more publications research somehow involving postcards.

to a Randall Rhoades of Ashland, Ohio, and was proposed around 1930.[5] The German equivalent is the undisputed, yet also not very common term *Philokartie*, and apparently rooted in the French special journal „Le Philocartiste".[6] Here, the semblance to philately is obvious. Often researchers seem to prefer "postcard research" instead of "deltiology". Such in terminological indecision might further hint towards a lack of scholarly consolidation. Yet, it appears a number of studies try to push in this direction. At disciplinary margins, postcards seem to find niches across cultural,[7] geographical,[8] regional,[9] historical,[10] and media

5   Smaridge, Norah, "Would You Pay $150 for a Postcard?", *New York Times*, May 16, 1976; p. 95.

6   Formely known as *La Cartophilie Illustrée* the journal relaunched as *Le Philocartiste. Moniteur des collectionneurs de cartes postales illustrées* in August 1903. See: Carline, Richard, *Pictures in the Post*, London, Gordon Fraser, 1971; p. 124.

7   Kaden, Ben, "Kinoarchitektur im Spiegel der DDR-Philokartie", in: Plaul, Marcus; Haumann, Anna-Rosa; Kröger, Kathleen (eds.), *Kino in der DDR. Perspektiven auf ein alltagsgeschichtliches Phänomen*, Baden-Baden, Nomos, 2022; p. 51–88; Baldwin, Brooke, "On the Verso: Postcard Messages as a Key to Popular Prejudices", *The Journal of Popular Culture* 22/3, 1988; p. 15–28. DOI: 10.1111/j.0022-3840.1988.2203.

8   Arreola, Daniel D.; Burkhart, Nick, "Photographic Postcards and Visual Urban Landscape", *Urban Geography*, 31/7, 2013; p. 885–904, DOI: 10.2747/0272-3638.31.7.885.

9   For example, the cultural geographer Daniel D. Arreola published quite a number of books on the depiction of the Mexican American borderlands in vintage postcards. Arreola, Daniel D., *Postcards from the Baja California border portraying townscape and place, 1900s-1950s*, Tucson, University of Arizona Press, 2021; Ibid., *Postcards from the Río Bravo Border: Picturing the Place, Placing the Pictures*, Austin, University of Texas Press, 2021.

10   Wilson, Kenneth, *Snapshots and short notes: images and messages of early twentieth-century photo postcards*, Denton, University of North Texas Press, 2020; Burns, Peter M., "Six postcards from Arabia: A visual discourse of colonial travels in the Orient", *Tourist Studies*, 2004/3; p. 187–303. DOI: 10.1177/1468797604057327.

studies,[11] and ethnographic research[12] or sometimes simply descriptive auto-ethnographic rediscoveries of their joys and potentials.[13] Each of those attempts is worthwhile and interesting. Yet, the scattering over time and disciplines once more empirically underlines a marginality of postcard studies, which probably comes for a reason. At first glimpse, postcards appear just somehow overlooked, still easy to handle.

Fig. 47: Mumbai, in the 1960s. The words "Finlays Fabrics" and "Congress" emerge from this urban view and suggest the economic and political reality of Independent India.

But when the actual handling starts, everything turns out to be more complicated than imagined. Or as Jan-Ola Östman puts it, postcards appear as a "paradoxical phenomenon, does not fit nicely into the tradi-

---

11   Östman, Jan-Ola, "The postcard as media", *Text & Talk*, 2004/3; p. 423–442. DOI: 10.1515/text.2004.017; Cure, Monica, *Picturing the postcard: a new media crisis at the turn of the century*, Minneapolis, University of Minnesota Press, 2018; Meikle, Jeffrey, *Postcard America: Curt Teich and the Imaging of a Nation, 1931–1950*, Austin, University of Texas Press, 2016.

12   Gugganig; Schor, *op.cit.*

13   Pyne, *op.cit.*

tional categories that scholars have devised as tools to get a better handle on social phenomena."[14]

They are, as Mascha Gugganig and Sophie Schor write, "an open system, with its various material and discursive dimensions." Yet, "[p]laying with these dimensions bears much potential for creating new methodical approaches, and potentially new genres." Which is exactly what I will exemplify in this article.

Postcards and visual urban research

I choose the research angle of visual urban research as it is probably the most prone field for sourcing postcards as material. To state the obvious:" Postcard imagery holds great promise as a resource for urban researchers."[15] When it comes to reaching a broader audience the depiction, perception, and visual interpretation of urban space has a lot of charm, as, for instance, three volumes by Ulrich Brinkmann alone exemplify.[16] Other examples showcase particular collections.[17] In many

---

14   Östman, *op.cit.*; p. 437.

15   Arreola; Burkhart; *op.cit.* The field of tourism might appear equally relatable to postcard studies. See: Modlin, Arnold E., "A market or "a relic of barbarism?" Toward a more inclusive analysis of social memory on postcards", in: Hanna, Stephen P.; Potter, Amy E.; *et al.* (eds.), *Social Memory and Heritage Tourism Methodologies*, London, Routledge, 2015; p. 170–188; Milman, Ady, "Postcards as representation of a destination image: The case of Berlin", *Journal of Vacation Marketing*, 2011/2; p. 157–170. DOI: 10.1177/1356766711435975.

16   Brinkmann, Ulrich, *Achtung vor dem Blumenkübel! Die Fußgängerzonen als Element des Städtebaus: Ansichtspostkarten in Ost- und Westdeutschland 1949 bis 1989*, Berlin, DOM, 2020; Ibid., *Matera moderna: Postkarten aus der Zeit des italienischen Wirtschaftswunders*, Berlin, DOM, 2022; Ibid., *Vorsicht auf dem Wendehammer! Die Straße als Element des Städtebaus: Ansichtspostkarten in der DDR und Bundesrepublik 1949 bis 1989*, Berlin, DOM, 2023.

17   Kramer, Thomas, *New York auf Postkarten. Die Sammlung Andreas Adam*, Zürich, Scheidegger & Spiess, 2010; Wagener, Wolfgang; Erganian, Leslie, *NEW WEST*, Munich, Hirmer, 2019.

cases, though not all, locality marks the collection's focus. Thus, displaying particular places all through the yesteryears using postcards can be potentially presented in countless iterations.[18] An interesting variation of the genre comes from the sociologist Renaud Epstein,[19] who specializes in cards depicting so-called "Zones à urbaniser en priorité"[20] and managed to build a large followership at his dedicated "Un jour, une ZUP, une carte postale"-Twitter-channel.[21] The appeal, undeniably, works. A rare, early, and more deltiological approach stems from the architect Alvin Boyarsky, whose "Chicago à la Carte" was published as a "florilegium" in a reader compiled in his memory.[22] His son Nicholas Boyarsky endeavored to extend his father's 1970s ideas towards a "deltiology of practice."[23] in order to use the medium to deliberate about built environments.[24]

Most of the books include essays or short texts to contextualize the material and elaborate on postcards and postcard history. Many state a perceived general disregard towards the potentials of the medium and accordingly mirror the introduction notes of many scholarly papers, once again, rediscovering the medium. Alas, few of these texts propose systematic insights into a methodology of postcard research. It seems

---

18 Schröter, Erasmus, *Bild der Heimat. Die Echt-Foto-Postkarten aus der DDR*, Berlin, Schwarzkopf und Schwarzkopf, 2002; Długosz, Mikolaj, *Latem w mieście: Summer in the city*, Warszawa, Fundacja Nowej Kultury Bęc Zmiana, 2016; Schlatter, Beat, *Postcards*, Basel, Christoph Merian Verlag, 2020; Thomson, David, *Dry Hole*, London, Mörel, 2022.

19 Epstein, Renaud, *On est bien arrivés: un tour de France des grands ensembles*, Paris, Le Nouvel Attila, 2022.

20 Bancilhon, Philippe; Monnier, Gérard, *Les années ZUP. Architectures de la croissance: 1960–1973*, Paris, Picard, 2002.

21 URL: https://twitter.com/renaud_epstein.

22 Boyarsky, Nicholas, *Serious Play. A Deltiology of Practice*, Melbourne, RMIT University, 2016. https://researchrepository.rmit.edu.au/esploro/outputs/doctoral/Serious-play-A-deltiology-of-practice/9921863895001341.

23 *Ibid.*

24 Boyarsky, Nicholas, "The Ephemeral Imagination. The Postcard and Construction of Urban Memory", *CANDIDE*, 2021/12; p. 73–85.

safe to say, that a methodological examination of an integrated deltio-logical method for architectural and urban studies so far remains largely cursory. Even where a certain wish to go deeper is stated, postcard im-ages are mostly used to source images and to illustrate. Sometimes they are utilized as scholarly proof. Only rarely they are considered as a medium with singular qualities beyond a specific use case. Except, of course, the studies focus deeper on postcards themselves.[25] Does this matter? In many cases, I'm inclined to say, it does not. An interesting study such as the one presented by Sangeeta and Ratnesh Mathur with their comprehensive and deeply researched presentation of Indian post-cards before 1947,[26] probably wouldn't gain anything in an additional reflection about a deltiological methodology.

Fig. 48: Mumbai. This rare representation of the Esso building (now Petrol House) shows a projection of the building completed in 1956. The collage technique evokes the practices of the interwar European avant-gardes.

25   Meikle, Jeffrey, *Postcard America, op.cit.*

26   Mathur, Sangeeta; Mathur, Rathnesh, *Picturesque India: A Journey in Early Picture Postcards (1896–1947)*, New Delhi, Niyhogi Books, 2018.

The impressive volume basically tells the story of India's modernization and industrialization while compiling a trove of information regarding the postcard production history of India. It does what it does and is in itself a seminal work both, for the postcard history of India and the history of postcards in India. Still, for my text, I want to take a different route.

Collecting images

Image programs and pictorial languages of picture postcards are extremely varied and in this a blessing and a curse. Postcard imagery documents phenomena relevant to social or cultural history in astonishing ramifications and breadth of motifs. There is hardly anything depictable that wasn't depicted on a postcard. Postcard images are "snippets that offer a cultural history that can't be found through other media and material culture."[27] But at the same instant they are almost impossible to overview in total. There is no comprehensive catalog for picture postcards and even the highly specified topical lists some collectors for certain topics are usually riddled with omissions. While extensive lists index about every type and variation of postage stamp that ever circulated, and even those that did not, no equivalent for postcards exists. Every postcard publicly indexed is one that more or less as fortuitously as by chance landed in an inventory of a collector willing to do so.[28]

Pictures on postcards were in demand as collector's items from the start and accordingly discussed and admired in clubs and magazines.[29] They sold well, so many publishers and even individuals put out enor-

---

27   Pyne; *op.cit.*

28   Judging by the online index collect there are suprisingly few collectors who actually are, at least publicly. https://colnect.com/de/postcards.

29   Cure, *op.cit.*; especially p. 157ff.; Carline, *op.cit.*; p. 63–72.

mous numbers and variations.[30] Ubiquitous availability, low barriers to entry, comparatively little space, and the infinite variety of motifs and thus starting points for thematic collections popularized collecting postcards as a hobby.[31] In addition, growing into diachronic testimonies of certain views and places over time,[32] postcards function perfectly as low-threshold tokens for nostalgia.[33] Knowing they were produced and handled in specific past timeframes gives them a particular aura. A postcard depicting a place in a certain moment often means, that the object at hand once actually might have been present at this place and around this time. Legible postmarks count as definite proof. In this regard, postcards are tangible time capsules. Postcards with urban and architectural motifs dominate throughout and in typological specifity,[34] but are particularly common, where places, spaces, and buildings were considered a special feature of the locality, i.e. usually new and/or more representative buildings. With the early 20th century's postcard boom, the need for broad marketing and therefore broad geographical coverage arose.[35] Often, the particular representative entity of a place, as in many cases came down to the church, market, court, post office, library, or simply a generic view down the main street. Messages were also diverse, yet often limited in expression by the constraints of mediality and social convention.[36] In earlier days, writing postcards was somehow controversial and innovative, particularly because of the quasi-public character of the medium.[37] For different and understandable reasons most collectors

30   See for instance on the "Postcard Mania" starting in the USA around 1898. Meikle, *op.cit.*; p. 14–16.
31   Kearns, Seamus, "Collecting Picture Postcards", *Dublin Historical Record*, 2001/2; p. 139–144.
32   Arreola; Burkhart; *op.cit.*
33   Martinovic, Dimitrije, *The Skin of Nostalgia: A Reflection on the Artifice of Postcards, Structuralist Filmmaking, and Home Movies*, Toronto, York University, 2014. http://hdl.handle.net/10315/30249.
34   For example: Kaden, 2022; *op.cit.*
35   Meikle; *op.cit.*
36   Cure, *op.cit.*
37   *Ibid.*; Östman (*op.cit.*) also describes a "public-private gradience".

did and do not emphasize collecting by the message. Reading the communication of strangers feels intrusive and offers from a collector's perspective, little value. It is also difficult to mold an interesting angle for a
topical collection and any public display would feel more offensive than
impressive. Images prevail with the exception of persons that tap into
postal history for stamps and postmarks. Understandably, many collectors exclusively prioritized the motif.

*Fig. 49: Mumbai's Marine Drive waterfront boulevard
is one of the most reproduced postcard motifs of India.
Comparing the views allows us to see the changes in
the urban landscape from the 1940s to the present day.*

Researching images (and messages)

As for research, there are also hints of deltiology as a form of hobbyist
research, now called citizen science. A 1975 article in the New York Times
quotes a collector named Dorothy Bloodgood as emphasizing: "Collecting postcards is a study of history and geography".[38] Unlike philately,
it was only able to establish itself to a limited extent during the 20th

---

38   Jailer, Mildred, "Yesterday's Postcards Are Today's New Treasures", *New York
Times*, Nov. 23, 1975; p. 82.

century. To this day, it is regularly rediscovered and more than less as a curiosity.[39] This partly resonates with Östman's assessments of "postcard[s] as a marginal, marginalized, and marginalizable phenomenon in society at large" that "looked down upon, frowned upon, and talked about pejoratively ",[40] though personally, I wouldn't agree completely. Often, I experience quite the opposite. Then again, nowadays the postcard's role might be so diminished, that we are already past any point of judgment and most people do not care at all, while those who do, differentiate more.

While topological postcards are of obvious relevancy for visual urban studies, messages can be too.[41] Of course, the field's deltiologists covet a certain type of message, i.e. scribbled perceptions of places. However, while such notes are not exactly rare, they are seldom detailed. In fact, it is very challenging to compile a workable corpus for an analysis that goes beyond anecdotal musings with the length of a tweet. Generally, postcards are very easy to collect. At least up to a certain moment in postal history, they accumulated almost inevitably on shelves or fridges. Some specimens are harder to find, but if one is not too picky, the nature of a batch product leaves enough copies out there to amass an exhaustive collection very fast with comparably low investment. Vendors describe postcards based on the imprinted descriptions; hence it is easy to search (online) for particular places or motifs. It becomes more difficult, though, if one is looking for a specific style, photographer, or year since that information is often lacking. It gets impossible in regard to messages. Any of those entered my collection purely by coincidence. Any indexing, order, and selection by messages start subsequently after acqui-

---

39   Smaridge, *op.cit.*; Correal, Annie, *The Postcard People Carry On*, New York Times, Jan. 27, 2018, Section MB; p. 1. https://www.nytimes.com/2018/01/26/nyregio n/postcard-people.html; Evelyn, Freja, "A collector was 'bitten by the postcard bug' 80 years ago; see some of his favorites", *The Picture Show: PHOTO STORIES FROM NPR.* Jan. 9, 2023. https://www.npr.org/sections/pictureshow/2023/01/o 9/1133372930/postcard-collector-donald-brown-amassed-hundreds-of-thousa nds-over-eight-decades.
40   Östman; *op.cit.*
41   Boyarski; *op.cit.*

sition and can only draw from the given material. Thus, there are plenty of misses and significantly fewer hits in looking for interesting text-image-relations. But from time to time there are. Nicholas Boyarsky provides some examples.[42] I will do too below.

Postcards as social media

Whenever there is a message on a picture postcard, two things emerge. First, relations between image and text. An image is either referenced or it is not. Both states are relational. Second, there are social traces. In terms of the unique features of picture postcards, neither the image nor the message alone suffices. Being fixed to the same material object in a literal double-sidedness is the crucial quality as well as the intentional mailability of picture postcards. Thus, this is what any deltiological method will center around.

Social (texts)

The *social* is as inherent to any form of deltiological study. Other than letters, which split into notepaper and envelope, posted postcards always come with their message and most of the times a variety of processing marks attached. Hence, they can be read as social as well as technical. For our cause, the technical turns out to be advantageous. Due to the requirement of being mailable, recto and verso of postcards are mostly standardized and provide a fixed frame for any variability. Object-wise, those standards make postcards easy to use, collect, handle, store, digitize, and possibly engage with. Even when leaving any message related narrative out, a postcard is already a social object. It is intended to be seen, bought, used, and received by a person. A mailed postcard is inevitably a social and extremely personal artifact: "Sending the

---

42   *Ibid.*

postcard is about representing yourself in a particular social and geographic space."[43] Given the inherently social, the deltiological method would aim to define, extract, compare, and analyze those social qualities of a postcard. Alternatively, one could speak of *reading* the different layers as social text. As with all professional reading and even more with the usual limitations on background information regarding the persons originally involved, reading means contextualizing: How does what I get from a card, relate to something else and what does it mean, or what can I deduct from it? Thus, a postcard's different peculiarities—image, imprints, publisher information, dates, message narrative, addressing, writtenness,[44] postal marks, possibly material blemishes and damages, annotations, collecting specific property markings—can be used as analytical points for reference.

Contexts

To read postcards scholarly, those particularities would need to be set in relation to the larger contexts. Since those are extensive, deltiology connects to a wide range of research topics, as the many though scattered attempts in different fields emphasize. Differentiating the specific technical, mediological, visual, and social qualities of picture postcards allows for determining certain analyzable basic features as well as additional technical, economical, and social context settings of the medium.[45] Such a deltiological baseline makes postcards approachable in a more structured and systematic way, as there are now reliable reference features. For instance, drawing from well-defined basic properties of pictures on postcards a comparative picture analysis of postcard photography could provide insights into different, socially shaped ways of seeing and depicting. And it would allow the question of whether

---

43   Jason, Farman quoted in: Pyne, *op.cit.*; p. 38.
44   Gillen; *op.cit.*
45   Prochaska, David, "Thinking Postcards", *Visual Resources: An International Journal of Documentation*, 2011; p. 383–99, DOI: 10.1080/01973762.2001.9658604.

there was (and is) a specific form of "postcard photography".[46] Hence, I suggest distinguishing *material qualities* and *contextual qualities* which both constitute picture postcards as research objects. A deltiological method, or in the end maybe just *deltiology*, would engage with identifying, understanding, describing, and refining those categories in order to link them to topical research questions, which do not necessarily have to center picture postcards. From a sociological or linguistical perspective, one could for instance compare messaging patterns of different forms of written personal communication to those extracted from postcards.[47] From a visual urban research perspective, comparing how particular buildings are depicted diachronically could pose a crucial research question.[48] In short: given fixed points of reference, postcards, especially used ones, bear a rich potential for research. They are both image and communication archives. Nevertheless, there are drawbacks: diversity in motifs and specimens and sheer quantity make a definite assessment of the potential difficult if not impossible. Even worse, any used postcard is an exclusive object. Studying postcards almost always turns into a lesson in contingency. Fortunately, as I will describe below, digitization might come to rescue.

Applied deltiological city scaping: every building on the Karl-Marx-Allee

For text-image relations on postcards, there are two possibilities: an explicit relation exists. Or it doesn't. If there is one, for visual urban research, a strong and elaborately written connection to the image is cov-

---

46   See for instance: Nicholas Boyarsky's study of Walker Evans' photography in relation to postcards. Boyarski, *op.cit.* Walker Evans was in fact himself an avid postcard collector; see: Rosenheim, Jeff, *Walker Evans and the picture postcard*, Göttingen, Steidl, 2009. There is also a whole chapter on "Researching Postcard Photographers" in: Bogdan, Robert; Weseloh, Todd, *Real Photo Postcard Guide: The People's Photograpy*, New York, Syracuse University Press, 2006; p. 195–20.

47   Gillen; *op.cit.*

48   Arreola, Burkhart; *op.cit.*

eted. In real life, it is surprisingly rare. Many relational statements are simple, and often more tacit than not: *This is where I am right now.* Yet, there are intriguing pieces. Reading those, potentials for deeper analysis becomes evident. In a presentation called, with a nod to artist Ed Ruscha, "Every Building in the Karl-Marx-Allee" I spoke on deltiology as a form of "visual urban research".[49] I argued that postcards are visual media AND memory media AND media objects at the same time, in fact with the same object. Such a triplet of states allows a threefold and often interwoven reading. First, a postcard can be read visually, including the whole methodological scope of Bildwissenschaft,[50] visual studies, and even art history. Picture postcard photography conceptionally oscillates between vernacular, documentary, and sometimes even artistic photography, making it an apt research object for photography theories between, well, Barthes[51] and Bourdieu.[52]

Reading the image

Collected according to certain criteria for instance a single street, postcards can serve as a diachronic research corpus on the presentation and perception of architecture, urban space, and the experience of place over time. For "Every Building on the Karl-Marx-Allee" I attempted to assemble a line-up of postcards depicting every newly built edifice of Berlin's grand socialist boulevard. Karl-Marx-Allee was constructed starting in the early 1950s in two construction phases each characterized by a specific socialist style of architectural aesthetics: the so-called National Tradition and the Ostmoderne.

49   Kaden, Ben, "Every Building on the Karl-Marx-Allee. Ansichtskarten als Quellen zur Architekturgeschichte der DDR", Berlin, Digitaler Dialog "Auf dem Weg zum Welterbe", Sep. 9, 2021.
50   https://en.wikipedia.org/wiki/Bildwissenschaft (02.03.2023).
51   Barthes, Roland, *Camera lucida. Reflections on photography* (1980), New York, Hill and Wang, 2010.
52   Boltanski, Luc; Bourdieu, Pierre; Castel, Robert, *Eine illegitime Kunst: die sozialen Gebrauchsweisen der Fotografie*, Hamburg, Europäische Verlagsanstalt, 2014.

Fig. 50: Picture postcard, circa 1955 Berlin Stalinallee
Liz.-Nr. A 110/55.

Ironically and not as planned, two rather pedestrian prefab blocks appeared later. Therefore, the street pretty much summarizes the architectural history of the GDR from the 1950s to the late 1970s. Given a name change after ten years from Stalinallee to Karl-Marx-Allee, it also onomastically opens up a door to the drifts and struggles of the place-related commemorative culture of the GDR. To this day, the boulevard, as shown on the postcard, succeeds in being impressive in its narrative. Even if one does not know any details, the impetus of representation is obvious. The space is wide open, the buildings shine, and are well proportioned. Greenery gives a placid atmosphere, mirrored in the strolls of the passers-by. Unexpected for such a metropolitan setting, no car traffic is in sight.

The mid-1950s card depicts the so-called Block-C with the penthouse the architect, Richard Paulick, designed for himself in the upper left corner.[53] The block was finished just a few years before and was one of the most ambitious and showy living quarters in East Berlin of the

53   Barz, Andreas; Dolff-Bonekämper, Gabi, "Das Haus auf dem Haus", in: Flierl, Thomas (ed.), *Bauhaus, Shanghai, Stalinallee, Ha-Neu: der Lebensweg des Architekten Richard Paulick 1903–1979*, Berlin, Lukas Verlag, 2020.

time. Tenants were either rewarded for outstanding achievements or luckily winning a raffle. The perspective leads eastbound down to the still-under-construction left tower of Frankfurter Tor, a major ensemble of GDR architecture designed by Hermann Henselmann and alluding to the churches at Berlin's historically central square Gendarmenmarkt, at the same time already expressing slight changes in the architectural idiom compared to the earlier planning. The prominent streetlamps were designed specifically for the street, also by Richard Paulick.[54]

Fig. 51: Embassy of BRD in New Delhi (1962), whose construction (1954–62) began at the same time as the Stalinallee in East Berlin was being built.

The street space visible cuts out the traffic and reminds us, how the boulevard actually has the width of two large streets combined. The image thus shows and condenses the architectural state of the GDR in the 1950s into a thick, yet easily decipherable pictorial text.

---

54   Oberpichler, Anja W., *Die Straßenbeleuchtung am Strausberger Platz und im II. Bauabschnitt der Karl-Marx-Allee zwischen Strausberger Platz und Alexanderplatz*, Berlin, Senatsverwaltung für Stadtentwicklung und Umwelt, 2014.

Reading the message

Fig. 52: Reverse side of the Stalinallee postcard (Fig. 50).

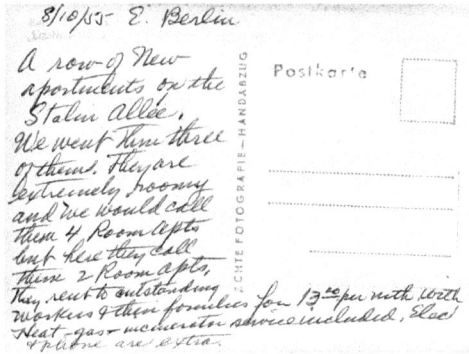

Turning the card even further charges the object with history. We are missing the backstory, but we still find a lot of information in the handwritten message on the back of the used but not mailed postcard. It reads like a descriptive memo, possibly for later presentation, and is arguably written by an American visitor, who could freely explore the eastern part of Berlin following the Four Power Agreement. From the sound of the message, however, it seems to be a recollection of facts provided during an official tour. The person notes almost as if adding an elaborate caption: "A row of New apartments on the Stalinallee. We went [into] three of them. They are extremely roomy and we would call them 4 Room apts but here they call them 2 Room apts, They rent to outstanding workers & their families [...]" Data and place are added: 8th of October 1955 in East Berlin. The date itself is significant, as October 7th was a national holiday to celebrate, in this case, the sixth anniversary of the GDR. In fact, the local Berliner Zeitung published an article on this day, that appears to echo the message written on the postcard in highlighting the quality of the new apartments.[55]

Reading the object

The real-photo postcard is in very good material condition and has the size of a photo print any studio could produce. Accordingly, the sloppily stamped information "ECHTE FOTOGRAFIE – HANDABZUG" reveals, that this particular card was actually produced in a photo lab and hence probably in a small batch. There is no information regarding a publisher. The card might have been made just for the occasion. Seeing the division and information on the back stamped and not printed supports this assumption.The quality of the print itself is good and sharp except for some blurry spots in the corner. There is an additional stamp in the upper left corner above the message showing an assigned licensing number. Even a more informal card such as this needed to be registered in the GDR. It also captions the card with the locality: *Berlin, Stalinallee*. Another visible property refers to what Julia Gillen introduced as "writtenness"[56] and "regulation of space".[57] Here, the handwriting is somehow idiosyncratic but still easy to read. Given the motif, place, setting, and message, the fact that it is written in English makes it stand out. It unnecessarily respects the division and the address field, only to digress at the bottom, which suggests a spontaneous scribbling. The provenance of the object could offer some additional clues. Unfortunately, I only remember that

---

55   Ke. [Berliner Zeitung], 1955.
56   She references Theresa Lillis' seven aspects of writing: "inscription, acts of mark-making; semiotic practice, the use of symbols appropriated through cultural-historical understandings; materiality, according to technological resources available; multimodality, both in the graphic design of the message and relation to the picture; mobility across time and space; a range of social and communicative functions; instantiations of social practice.". Lillis, Theresa, *The Sociolinguistics of Writing*, Edinburgh, Edinburgh University Press, 2013.
57   Gillen; *op.cit.*

the card was sold online by a vendor in the USA. Hence, at least it is verifiable that the card made it from Berlin to the USA.

But: not every message on the Karl-Marx-Allee (collecting contingency)

While it turns out to be surprisingly easy to visually reconceptualize both sides of an urban boulevard using picture postcards, the example might be a double exception. Firstly, not every street or place was documented that extensive, so the approach fits best for the showcases of urbanism or tourist hotspots. Secondly, as described, the specificity of postcards not solely lies in the image.[58] Yet, it is about potentially using the card for communication. As said above, messages expressively referencing the image are comparably infrequent. But that's not all. Most of those are also undiscoverable and inaccessible, hidden in private collections or overlooked in storage. No one else can own this particular specimen, neatly tucked away in my private black box labelled "Berlin-Friedrichshain". When compiling corpora using customary channels of acquisitions, vendors, online retailers, flea markets, in regard to messages one has to still rely on chance findings. As postcards were intendedly short-lived and in fact often vanished, one mostly has to deal with a motley stack of more or less accidental survivors, dispersed even further by collectors picking and leaving certain cards. Hence, corpora will necessarily remain fragmentary. While online shops index by motif, messages are almost never seen as something of interest. And even if they were, there are no agreements on how to index. Empirically, even in plentiful collections, many messages may turn out to be rather redundant birthday wishes and holiday greetings with an odd gem here or there. Since postcards are necessarily semi-public,[59] most people stuck to letters for their more personal and elaborate correspondence.

---

58   Though there can be something as specific research on photography for postcards, see for instance Bogdan; Weseloh; *op.cit.*

59   Östman; *op.cit.*

However, "all messages have the potential to provide insight into how the cards were used and about the people who used them."[60] But extracting and contextualizing such insights, however, remains challenging, as even detailed and intriguing texts often lack sufficient context information to draw substantive conclusions. In many cases, there is a lot of guesswork involved. Therefore, the short messages somehow mirror properties of the images: They are curt starting points for contextualization, fragments, and snippets of the actual settings. This is not necessarily a bad thing. But it demands a different epistemological approach, one that is accepting and managing this kind of incompleteness and contingency. Yet, the question remains: how to operationalize a deltiological method?

Image, message, object—reading is fundamental

Above, I suggested a kind of semiotic approach based on three paths of reading: the image, the message, and the object. In short, to read the image means to analyze the picture, its object, style, composition, technique, and anything that is shown and how it is depicted. Particular details can be inventoried, described, and analyzed separately. Context can be added. For presentations, I often magnify sections of interest.[61] Reading the message, therefore, focuses on the content of the message and its contextualization. It means analyzing any object-related properties and, if possible, contexts as well. However, scholarly reading always needs a lens, usually cut by particular research interests. In a very original and specific paper Nicholas Boyarski, for instance, accesses the role of picture postcards in regard to the "construction of urban memory."[62] He identifies underlying "themes and questions"

---

60   Bogdan; Weseloh; *op.cit.*

61   For an example see: https://benkaden.tumblr.com/post/706148230587645952/ansichtskarte-berlin-stalinallee-t-89058-rnr (02.03.2023).

62   Boyarski; *op.cit.*

regarding "collecting and reading of the postcard", all of which refer to discourses[63]:

1. "the discourses between the individual and the city"
2. "[the discourses] between the formal and the informal"
3. "[the discourses] between the sedentary and the nomadic"
4. "[the discourses] between urbanism and micro-urbanism".

Östman also pointed out the potentiality and the challenges of postcards for discourse analysis itself.[64] While postcards appear very promising at first, they are actually hard to operationalize. In fact, they turn out being difficult to categorize and to address with the established scholarly "tools of analysis". Defining particular topical categories, as Boyarski did, appears at least to be a basic step, while of course leaving the problem of contingency. Now, in terms of conceptualizing multimodality, another variable could be introduced to integrate the social dimension even further. As the proposed deltiological method tends to be a semiotic examination aimed to uncover the form, semantics, and maybe intentions related to postcards, one could argue within this constellation image captions and addresses fulfill a somewhat similar role. While captions refer to what is depicted, any address refers to a person involved. Even when on postcards sender's addresses are uncommon, receiver's addresses are in most cases present and can reveal much information, especially when analyzed in relation to the message. With a corpus large enough, there could be a chance for modeling social networks down to an interpersonal level using this data.[65]

---

63   *Ibid.*; p. 85.
64   Östman, *op.cit.*; p. 438.
65   Privacy rules, of course, apply.

Legal limitations

Obviously, privacy law and research ethics raise important issues that limit such an approach and need to be cleared first. But to begin with, for instance, place-to-place analysis and the nature and changes in mail traffic could be already addressed. For images, copyright can be equally complicated. Images are copyrightable works. At the same time, empirically today most vintage postcards would count under orphan works.[66] Therefore, copyright clearance in itself would in many cases come down already to deltiological research. Some legal regimes provide different exceptions for research such as fair use, or fair dealing, but to varying degrees, thus complicating things even further. This also affects any expectations towards mass digitization and datafication for building relevant corpora and opening them up for scholarly or even public use. If in doubt, the motto in research might be: tell, don't show. Yet, it does not apply to the body of public domain postcards. As with many source materials for digital research, we probably need to accept a moving time wall and start with the very vintages.

Digitization (Postcards as digital research material)

As used postcards are unique by nature, in pre-digital times building an encroaching corpus seemed nearly impossible. Contingency dominated. Findability was an issue. Image-based collection building was less complicated since there were copies available. For message analysis there is no way around going big data, i.e. amassing a preferably large corpus in order to then narrow it down again to a sample of relevant specimens. In digital research environments, postcard research might be reshuffled. Picture postcards can be mass digitized and indexed and turned into structured data sets representing collections accessible. searchable, and reusable. Of course, any digitized postcard becomes its own separate object and any tactile information must be coded as a quality of the

---

66   https://en.wikipedia.org/wiki/Orphan_work (02.03.2023).

respective data object too. Data modeling in general is not exactly triv-
ial, though the tangible constraints of the medium can be utilized for
these steps very well. Modeling multimodality, i.e. the different levels of
relationships embedded in the original as well as the new modes result-
ing from digital specifics is a different story. The same goes for linking
data elements across all objects contained in a corpus. Suddenly, deltiology enters the sphere of big data analytics and digital humanities. One
simple yet convincing presentation is provided by the Austrian National
Library. A project called AKON[67] explores ways of presenting the 75.000
topographical picture postcards in the library's holdings.[68] The available
solution uses georeferences to map the respective cards onto a zoomable
world map.[69] Unfortunately, additional non-topographical information
is only sparsely indexed. Nevertheless, AKON already demonstrates the
potential of digital deltiology. Given a yet-to-be-developed standardized
deltiological metadata scheme, one can easily imagine the value of integrating several collections in such a presentation, enabling multilayered
explorability. Of course, we are still talking about the images and some
formal properties such as publisher or year of production. But this again
would prepare a starting point for further steps of integrating the more
social properties of picture postcards as well. To go even further and connect with current trends, features to encode and annotate the various
written, pictorial, and social texts can be included. If open for citizen research, it would neatly loop back to deltiology as a field of passionate engagement for nearly anyone, just as it was at the height of the "postcard
mania".

---

67   "Ansichtskarten online"; https://akon.onb.ac.at/ (02.03.2023).

68   Müller, Christa; Mokre, Jan; Hintersonnleitner, Michael, "AKON – Ansichtskarten online", in: *Bibliothek – Forschung und Praxis*, 2017/42; DOI: 10.1515/bfp-2017-
0031.

69   https://akon.onb.ac.at/#center=eurypzpgxczb&zoom=3 (02.03.2023).

Summary

So if there was something such as a deltiological method, what could it be like?

Following my previous remarks, I propose a three-tier outline:

1. a bare-bone frame that defines the unique qualities of the medium postcard (and hence makes a method deltiological).
2. a set of applications that stem from a particular angle or research question and link those to the specifics of postcards.
3. topical analysis that necessarily breaches into other fields and is hence per se interdisciplinary.

Any of these can be broken down into separate elements, that can be read semiotically and contextualized. Given the specifics of a postcard, reading embraces the image, the message, and the object as an object. Since such a reading needs a defined scope in order to lead somewhere, a particular field of research provides the definition. Visual urban research is only one example. Myriads of other topical scopes are imaginable, too. In fact, as postcards probably depict every topical phenomenon from celebrities to war photography, they can be image-wise utilized for every thinkable topic. Message analysis might be more constrained given the limitations of the medium. Yet, there is a huge variety of forms of expression as well. There are not only waves of popularity of the medium but also shifts in usage patterns. Any deltiological research should contextualize those, too. The challenge remains to identify or built a conclusive corpus of material and develop research tools to explore it. In most cases, research will follow an already existing collection. In a perfect world, the collection would be digitized and datafied following open research standards to link it to other collections. While any postcard itself is a unique object, making postcards available and reusable in suitable cultural data infrastructures could update this mediological revolution of the 19th century into the 21st. And, not least, it could rekindle postcard passions and inspire new forms of re-materialization, too.

Coda: Happy New Year 1966

Fig. 53/54: Left: National Physical Laboratory, New Delhi (1956). Produced by the Advertising Branch, Ministry of I. & B.Govt. of India and issued by the Tourist Traffic Branch Ministry of Transport, Printed in India by the Times of India Press, Bombay. Right: Reverse side of the National Physical Laboratory postcard (Fig. 53).

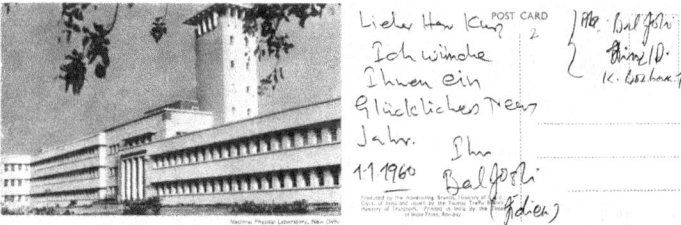

Looking at this postcard, there is at the same time vast and very little information. This paradoxical occurrence is not rare when it comes to cultural artifacts. As we have seen, the standardization of the medium helps extract a defined set of data from any given card. We have precisely one image and one message. Alas, in this case, we are again missing postal data. Though we get a sender's address, sadly this one is rather difficult to decipher. Personal communication comes with the idiosyncratic patterns of handwriting, an obstacle for OCR, and an ambivalence from the stance of deltiological ethics: Illegibility protects privacy. This postcard was never intended to persist for 60+ years and to serve as data for digitally mediated research. It is always a tense issue of how deep one might intrude into the usually personal communication. One may argue, postcards are not letters, hence by default open to read and people used them accordingly. Still, one comes across messages of endearment, grief, anger, or despair, that were never intended to enter a digitized corpus. And, of course, people usually regarded postcards as ephemeral, unaware of digital humanities research and suchlike reexamining communications a century later.

Scholarly curiosity is one thing. But deltiology also needs an informed yet empathic sensitivity on what to include in making material re-readable. When it comes to postcard images stemming from amateur and vernacular photography, the same applies to the pictures. Even if it is frustrating for research, public deltiology, which includes citizen research as well as artistic processing, needs to balance case by case what to include, what to show, and what to make reusable. A "happy new year", however, should be fine with everyone.

References

Arreola, Daniel D.; Burkhart, Nick, "Photographic Postcards and Visual Urban Landscape", *Urban Geography*, 31/7, 2013.

Bancilhon, Philippe; Monnier, Gérard, *Les années ZUP. Architectures de la croissance 1960–1973*, Paris, Picard, 2002.

Barthes, Roland, *Camera lucida. Reflections on photography* (1980), New York, Hill and Wang, 2010.

Bogdan, Robert; Weseloh, Todd, *Real Photo Postcard Guide*, New York, Syracuse University Press, 2006.

Boltanski, Luc; Bourdieu, Pierre; Castel, Robert, *Eine illegitime Kunst: die sozialen Gebrauchsweisen der Fotografie*, Hamburg, Europäische Verlagsanstalt, 2014.

Boyarski, Nicholas, "The Ephemeral Imagination. The Postcard and Construction of Urban Memory", *Candide*, 2021/12; p. 73–85.

Brinkmann, Ulrich, *Achtung vor dem Blumenkübel! Die Fußgängerzonen als Element des Städtebaus, Ansichtspostkarten in Ost- und Westdeutschland 1949 bis 1989*, Berlin, DOM, 2020.

Brinkmann, Ulrich, *Matera moderna: Postkarten aus der Zeit des italienischen Wirtschaftswunders*, Berlin, DOM, 2022.

Brinkmann, Ulrich, *Vorsicht auf dem Wendehammer! Die Straße als Element des Städtebaus. Ansichtspostkarten in der DDR und Bundesrepublik 1949 bis 1989*, Berlin, DOM, 2023.

Burns, Peter M., "Six postcards from Arabia: A visual discourse of colonial travels in the Orient", *Tourist Studies*, 2004/3; p. 187–303.

Carline, Richard, *Pictures in the Post*, London, Gordon Fraser, 1971.

Cure, Monica, *Picturing the postcard: a new media crisis at the turn of the century*, Minneapolis, University of Minnesota Press, 2018.

Epstein, Renaud, *On est bien arrivés : un tour de France des grands ensembles*, Paris, Le Nouvel Attila, 2022.

Flierl, Thomas (ed.), *Bauhaus, Shanghai, Stalinallee, Ha-Neu: der Lebensweg des Architekten Richard Paulick 1903–1979*, Berlin, Lukas Verlag, 2020.

Gillen, Julia, "Writing Edwardian postcards", *Journal of Sociolinguistics*, 2013/13; p. 488–521.

Gugganig, Mascha; Schor, Sophie, "Multimodal Ethnography in/of/as Postcards", *American Anthropolist* 122/3, 2020; p. 691–97.

Jailer, Mildred, "Yesterday's Postcards are today's new treasures", *New York Times*, Nov.23., 1975; p. 82.

Kaden, Ben, "'My Dear Mother' Multimodalität als Herausforderung bei der Auseinandersetzung mit Ansichtskarten", *Retraceblog*, 01.11.2021.

Kearns, Seamus, "Collecting Picture Postcards", *Dublin Historical Record*, 2001/2, p. 139–44.

Kramer, Thomas, *New York auf Postkarten. Die Sammlung Andreas Adam*, Zürich, Scheidegger & Spiess, 2010.

Liepach, Christoph; Kaden, Ben, *Gera ostmodern*, Leipzig, sphere publishers, 2020.

Mathur, Sangeeta; Mathur, Ratnesh, *Picturesque India: A Journey in Early Picture Postcards (1896–1947)*, New Delhi, Niyhogi Books, 2018.

Meikle, Jeffrey, *Postcard America: Curt Teich and the Imaging of a Nation, 1931–1950*, Austin, University of Texas Press, 2016.

Östman, Jan-Ola, "The postcards as media", *Text & Talk*, 2004/3; p. 423–42.

Plaul, Marcus; Haumann, Anna-Rosa; Kröger, Kathleen (eds.), *Kino in der DDR: Perspektiven auf ein alltagsgeschichtliches Phänomen*, Baden-Baden, Nomos, 2022.

Prochaska, David, "Thinking Postcards", *Visual Resources: An International Journal of Documentation*, 2011: p. 383–99.

Pyne, Lydia, *Postcards: The Rise and Fall of the World's First Social Network*, London, Reaktion Books, 2021

Rosenheim, Jeff, *Walter Evans and the picture postcard*, Göttingen, Steidl, 2009.

Schröter, Erasmus, *Bild der Heimat. Die Echt-Foto-Postkarten aus der DDR*, Berlin, Schwarzkopf und Schwarzkopf, 2002.

Wagener, Wolfgang; Erganian, Leslie, *NEW WEST*, Munich, Hirmer, 2019.

Wilson, Kenneth, *Snapshots and short notes: images and messages of early 20th-century photo postcards*, Denton, University of North Texas Press, 2020.

Framing Fragments
The Image, Modernity, and Architecture

Saptarshi Sanyal

Fig. 55: Mumbai, Marine Drive Boulevard in the 1960s.

The Image as a Site of Architectural Production

Architecture, we could say, might seem inseparable from its image. This essay reflects on such a relationship within the realm of writing *architectural* histories of modernity. Here, we could argue how the image operates as a site of consuming architecture through the photograph—which in a sense, is as integral to informing and producing knowledge of architecture as other key representative forms like drawing or writing. We may also speculate, even discover evidence of how often photographic images shape the practice of architectural designers.

The role such images, particularly photographs, play in historically situating and inscribing architecture seems far less questionable (for reasons to keep this text focussed on the material at hand, I'm conscious of leaving out from this discussion the moving image or motion picture, or for that matter the more current, virtual, modes of simulating spatial and architectural reality). Those writing about, describing, analysing, or lecturing on architecture often rely, rather than the actual artefact, on an object that represents it. They lean on visuals to speak about spaces they haven't walked through, sought refuge from the heat or cold in, felt the warmth of light or the cold of shadow within, surfaces they haven't touched. Seldom have they experienced architecture 'in the flesh', so to speak. Some conscientious architectural historians take exception to such an approach. To stay true to the "articles of the discipline", for instance, Reyner Banham impressed upon a research student in the 1980s—a student who later became the acclaimed scholar Adrian Forty—how a historian must write only about those buildings, spaces, or places s/he has seen or personally experienced.[1]

Yet, such a thing can be considered the privilege of those for whom international or intercontinental mobility is an easy affordance. Beyond those in post-imperial societies, the question of how accessible travel might be remains open. It is possible, for instance, to speculate about the asymmetries of how many visual bodies of work produced by Indian travellers and photographers travelling in Britain or Europe or America in the nineteenth or twentieth centuries, stack up against those of individuals and groups from such societies travelling to India. Or whether travellers from other post-colonial societies such as Indonesia or Vietnam have as much to say about the Dutch or French as the latter have to say about them. I will not get into these debates here. But the limits to transporting ourselves to the places or experiencing spaces and buildings we want to write about, far too many to describe, prompt our turn to the photograph. Today, in the age of social media, students, educators, practitioners, or even potential clients across the world might see

---

1   Forty, Adrian, *Concrete and culture: a material history*, London, Reaktion Books, 2012.

and 'experience' architecture on Instagram or Archdaily far more than in person. Historically thus, as in the present, the image of architecture emerging from the photograph and architecture itself are tied a dialogic relationship.

Yet, just as physical distance separates us from buildings and spaces we wish to think of or write about, so does time. Oddly, this temporal aspect equalises different constituencies, privileged travellers or not. Such a time-space distance proffers, to say the least, one of the prime openings for architectural histories to be written. Photographs are integral to negotiating such a distance—even if, as Walter Benjamin reminds us, in a photograph "something has actually to be *constructed*, something artificial, something set up" (emphasis in original).[2] It is in this sense that this essay reflects on the role the present collection of postcards from India. It reflects on the plural, fragmented and uneven nature of modernity as observed through the photographic image as a site of architectural production.

Fig. 56: Mumbai, Churchgate and the Eros Cinema in the 1970s.

---

2   Benjamin, Walter, "A short history of photography" (1931), *Screen*, vol. 13, no. 1, 1972; p.5–26.

Fragments and Fiction

In his seminal thesis, Kenneth Boulding reminds us that the image is a form of knowledge making that transcends what we witness. Reflecting on how such knowledge is rendered mutable through the "message [that] hits an image", Boulding argues that, when contested, images remain "resistant to change".[3] Collectively considered, the postcards we witness in this collection assert many kinds of change, however. They appear, again collectively, far from singular in the image they construct of architectural modernity in Indian cities. Individually straddling a staggering range of time, each visual fragment portrays not just the changing stylistic and spatial character of buildings, environments and spaces, but also photographic and representational techniques; the hand-painted, sometimes oversaturated, colours of the Taj Mahal Hotel or General Post Office (GPO) in Bombay, the Imperial Hotel and Ashoka Hotel in New Delhi, and the Kalighat Temple and pontoon bridge spanning the Hooghly in Calcutta are particularly conspicuous in this respect.

Specific photographs bear testimony to the resistance to change that the makers of such images might have experienced. The juxtaposition of colonial (and post-colonial) modernity with more indigenous modes of transport, for example, occupies the focal point of Bombay's GPO, the horse-drawn 'ekka',[4] as opposed to the European carriage. In Bombay itself, a lone pedestrian walks along a traffic median at Churchgate, offering a foreground to busy traffic surrounding a modernist edifice, ostensibly the offices of "Finlay's Fabrics". Bullock carts traverse the paved streets fronting the expansive 1800s-built Writers Buildings of Calcutta around the Holwell memorial, commemorating the sinister Black Hole

---

3   Boulding, Kenneth E., *The Image, Knowledge in Life and Society*, Ann Arbor, University of Michigan Press, 1956; p.7–8.

4   An 'ekka' is a two-seater vehicle drawn by a horse, as opposed to a multi-seater where the horse-driver and passengers are separated, the latter often occupying a compartment in the rear.

incident of the eighteenth century.[5] A bullock cart also appears in front of the elegant Crawford Market in Bombay. Some photographs also construct juxtapositions: the spherical, or onion-shaped domes dominating the images of a hybrid architectural setting, the mosque on Muhammad Ali Road, while also forming a backdrop (the Prince of Wales Museum), to the photograph of a modern automobile speeding past Durga Bajpai's understated Jehangir Art Gallery.

The indigenous denizens of these Indian metropolises seem to resist experiences of colonial and modernist architecture or respond to it with practical exigencies—an everyday resistance of inhabiting modern spaces, perhaps of the kind that Douglas Haynes and Gyan Prakash posit.[6] Conversely, counterparts from their erstwhile, racially dominant societies seem to cling to India's new-found architectural modernity in the post-colonial period. A couple of images take us, to recall Thorstein Veblen, into their world of conspicuous consumption,[7] a world of extravagant leisure within luxury hotels such as the Sun and Sand in Bombay or the Oberoi Inter-continental in New Delhi.

All such images are but fragments. But how do we interpret them? They appear to construct a fiction of Indian cities and environments resisting the onslaught of both colonial modernity and the architectural modernism that followed. Indian cities, their architectures, and the experiences of these cities and architectures, we are told through these photographs, did not yield so easily to the imperatives, perhaps also a fiction, of a universal modernity. Rather, they complicate the story. These spaces, buildings, and environments, seem to assert that modernity is hybrid and plural. Rather than a robust category applicable across cultures and societies, architecture meets its adversary in

---

5   Hill, S.C., *Indian Records' Series, Bengal in 1756–57*, Volume III, London, John Murray, 1905; p.131–53.

6   Haynes, Douglas; Prakash, Gyan (eds.), *Contesting Power: Resistance and Everyday Social Relations in South Asia*, Berkeley, University of California Press, 1991; p.1–22.

7   Veblen, Thorstein, *The Theory of the Leisure Class*, New York, B.W. Huebach, 1918; p. 68–101.

them. Domesticated by its many inhabitants, cities and architecture emerge as porous and leaky, both as conceptual and physical containers of modernity, also a kind of delicate bubble in which the conspicuous consumption of modernity is held by some.

The Photographic Gaze: From Above and Below

About half of the postcards of this collection view urban spaces from above. In their wide, sweeping view of the cityscape, we are compelled to recall Swati Chattopadhyay's critique of the grandiose, how "an aesthetics of big scale dominates our historical imagination".[8] Still, photographs of particular buildings, seen from the eye level, comprise a third of the collection. This brings us, finally, to two interrelated questions. What happens when we photograph buildings and urban spaces? Does the photograph, with its colours, forms, lights, details, animate our imagination and understanding of modern architecture?

Fig. 57: Kolkata, Brabourne Road in the 1960s.

---

8   Chattopadhyay, Swati, "Architectural History or a Geography of Small Spaces?", *Journal of the Society of Architectural Historians*, March 2022/1, vol. 81; p. 5–20.

Or do photographs, little more than a shadow of reality, deprive us of the rich lived experience of architecture and urbanisms? These questions bring us back to the mythology of the popular image, embodied in the very medium of the postcard, perhaps a mode of speech, a meta-language of symbols and meanings of architectural modernity.

Yet, it is this aspect of the popular image that ushers in fresh ways of looking at modernity through Indian architecture and its metropolises. Images exist in a triad: the site of their production, the sites of their consumption and those of their interpretation—domains that include the creator, receiver as well as the researcher. More importantly, the image, while very much embedded in a modern technology of photography and printing, defies easy classification. This collection of postcards subverts the ways in which India entered the colonial gaze as a form of unchanging knowledge where architecture and cities are concerned.[9] The very ambiguity of the image helps to transcend the colonial-modern impetus of labelling and classifying,[10] a problem that very much populates architectural histories to the present day.[11] In effect, such an image of Indian modernity—as experienced through this collection of postcards—brings forth varying, competing and not necessarily coherent, perspectives through its architectural and urban spaces, both from above and below.

References

Barthes, Roland, *Mythologies*, London, Vintage, 1993.
Benjamin, Walter, "A Short History of Photography" (1931), *Screen*, 13, no.1, 1972; p. 5–26.

---

9   Prakash, Gyan, *Another Reason: science and the imagination of modern India*, Princeton, Princeton University Press, 1999; p.21–22.

10   Chakrabarty, Dipesh, "Modernity and ethnicity in India", *South Asia: Journal of South Asian Studies*, vol. 17, no. 1, 1994; p.143–155.

11   Sanyal, Saptarshi, "The paradox of categories" (book review) *Architecture and Independence: The Search for Identity—India 1880 to 1980* by Lang, Jon; Desai, Madhavi; Desai, Miki, in: *Architectural Research Quarterly*, vol. 26, 2022/1; p.105–08.

Boulding, Kenneth E., *The Image, Knowledge in Life and Society*, 9th edn, Ann Arbor, University of Michigan Press, 1973.

Chakrabarty, Dipesh, "Modernity and Ethnicity in India", *South Asia: Journal of South Asian Studies*, 17, no.1, 1994; p. 143–55.

Chattopadhyay, Swati, "Architectural History or a Geography of Small Spaces?", *Journal of the Society of Architectural Historians*, vol. 81, no. 1, p. 5–20, 2022. https://doi.org/10.1525/jsah.2022.81.1.5

Forty, Adrian, *Concrete and Culture: A Material History*, London, Reaktion Books, 2012.

Haynes, Douglas; Prakash, Gyan (eds.), *Contesting Power: Resistance and Everyday Social Relations in South Asia*, Berkeley, University of California Press, 1991.

Hill, S. C., *Indian Records' Series, Bengal in 1756–57, Volume III*, London, John Murray, 1905.

Prakash, Gyan, *Another Reason: Science and the Imagination of Modern India*, Princeton, Princeton University Press, 1999.

Sanyal, Saptarshi, "The Paradox of Categories"—(Book Review) *Architecture and Independence: The Search for Identity—India 1880 to 1980* by Jon Lang, Desai Madhavi, Miki Desai, in: *Architectural Research Quarterly*, 26, no.1, p. 105–08, 2022. https://doi.org/10.1017/S1359135552200028 8

Veblen, Thorstein, *The Theory of the Leisure Class*, New York, B.W. Huebach, 1918.

Fig. 58/59: Left: Mumbai, Mahatma Gandhi Memorial, Sanjay Gandhi National Park, 1969. Right: Chennai, Valluvar Kottam, Memorial to Poet Saint Thiruvalluvar, 1976.

Fig. 60/61: Left: Agra, Clarks Shiraz, 1950s. Right: Claridge's Hotel, New Delhi, 1955.

List of figures

Authors

Éléonore Muhidine (b. 1988) completed her PhD in Architectural History at the Rennes University and the Free University in Berlin. She holds a Master's degree in Art History from the Paris 1 Panthéon-Sorbonne University and a Master's degree in History of Architecture from the Architecture School in Versailles, France. She works as a researcher at the School of Architecture in Potsdam and is affiliated researcher at the Zentrum Moderner Orient in Berlin. Her current research focuses on the architecture of the modern movement in India and on Indian architects during the 20th century. She is currently working on an architectural history of Bombay's cinemas 1900–1960 from the perspective of the city's urban history, as well as from a transnational perspective on cinema's architectural design. She recently published an article on the heritage of Mumbai's Marine Drive in the journal *Architectura* (2022/50, "Perspektiven der Forschung", eds. Barry Bergdoll, Andreas Schwarting, Klaus Tragbar), and two essays for the Mumbai Architecture Guide (Berlin, DOM Publishers) to be published in 2023.

Omar Khan is the author of *Paper Jewels Postcards from the Raj* (2018) and *From Kashmir to Kabul The Photographs of John Burke and William Baker 1860–1900* (2002). He grew up in Vienna, Austria and Islamabad, Pakistan and is a graduate of Dartmouth College, Columbia and Stanford universities. He lives in San Francisco where he works as Chief Technology Officer at the NGO Common Sense Media. He founded Harappa.com in 1995 and has researched early photography and ephemera of the subcontinent for over thirty years. A growing portion of his large postcard collection focused on South Asia is available at PaperJewels.org: https://www.paperjewels.org/

Preeti Chopra is professor of modern architecture, urban history and visual studies at the University of Wisconsin-Madison who specializes in the visual, spatial, and cultural landscapes of South Asia and the British empire. She trained as an architect (CEPT, Ahmedabad), landscape architect, urban planner, and architectural historian (University of California, Berkeley) and has conducted research in western and southern India. Chopra is the author of *A Joint Enterprise: Indian Elites and the Making of British Bombay* (Minneapolis, University of Minnesota Press, 2011). She is currently working on a second book on colonial Bombay. Chopra has published on a range of subjects that embraces charity and philanthropy, the naming of city districts, French colonial urbanism in Pondicherry, the formation of suburbs in Bombay, and art and memory in the Indian city. She has received numerous research grants and fellowships, including from the Institute for Research in the Humanities at the University of Wisconsin–Madison, the Netherlands Institute for Advanced Study in the Humanities and Social Sciences, Amsterdam, the International Institute of Asian Studies, Leiden and Centre d'Histoire, Sciences Po, Paris. She is the recipient of the 2023 Suzanne Deal Booth Rome Prize at the American Academy in Rome.

Anupam Bansal (b. 1969) is an architect, urbanist, and academician. He co-founded Atelier for Built-Environment Research & Design along with his partner Rajesh Dongre in 1996. Over the last two decades, they have built a diverse portfolio of projects ranging from Research Campuses, Universities, Schools, Cultural Institutions, Corporate Offices, Hospitals etc. to name a few. Many of their projects have received critical acclaim and awards, on National and International platforms. Anupam received his Bachelor of Architecture degree from School of Planning and Architecture, New Delhi in 1993, subsequently graduated in Master of Architecture from Kansas State University, Manhattan/USA in 1996. He has written and lectured on various aspects of the history and urban development of Delhi and India. He co-authored *The Delhi Architecture Guide* (Berlin, DOM Publishers) along with Malini Kochupillai. This well illustrated and mapped book is the first of its kind architectural guide of an Indian city, which covers the entire timeline of Delhi's architecture from Sultanate, Islamic, Mughal, Colonial and Post-Independence Modern and contemporary architecture. His other writings include 'Extending Imperial Delhi: the Diplomatic Enclave of Chanakyapuri', 'Housing Types And Their Evolution: Delhi 1900–2014', 'Pastiche Architecture: On the architectural Surges of Hafeez".

Shraddha Bhatawadekar (b. 1986) is an archaeologist and has been working in the field of heritage management and education. She completed her doctorate titled *A Place of Hybrid Encounters: Heritage Biography of a Railway Station. Story of Victoria Terminus*, now Chhatrapati Shivaji Maharaj Terminus, Mumbai in affiliation with the DFG-Research Training Group 1913 at the Brandenburg University of Technology, Cottbus-Senftenberg, Germany, where she is currently affiliated as a postdoctoral researcher. In her research, she focuses on the multi-layered dimensions of heritage, highlighting hybridity and transculturality. With the use of an object biography approach, she shows how the entanglement of place, people, objects, and meanings together constitute heritage. Shraddha Bhatawadekar is a recipient of Fulbright-Nehru Academic and Professional Excellence Fellowship (2015–16) and Alexander von Humboldt German Chancellor Fellowship (2016–17). She takes special interest in heritage education and outreach and has facilitated various courses and trainings.

Yves-Marie Rault-Chodankar (b. 1991) is a postdoctoral researcher at the Institut Francilien Recherche Innovation Société (IFRIS) in France. He has completed his doctorate in Development Geography at the Université de Paris. His PhD thesis looked at the globalization of India's pharmaceutical industry, with a focus on the industrial role of Mumbai. He has been a visiting scholar and guest lecturer at the Tata Institute of Social Science in Mumbai. He lives between France and India and conducts research on industrial dynamics and regional development in the Global

South. His research focuses on economic development and technological globalization and has been published in leading international journals such as *Social Science* and Medicine and the *Journal of Economic Geography*.

Ben Kaden studied library science, sociology, and political science at Humboldt-Universität zu Berlin. He is interested in the relationships between spatial representation and perception, memory culture, and (postcard) photography. In 2020, he published *Karten zur Ostmoderne* (Leipzig, Sphere Publishers), in which he examined picture postcards depicting urban settings and architecture of the GDR. He regularly writes about picture postcards with library motifs for the open-access journal LIBREAS.

Saptarshi Sanyal (b.1983) is an architectural historian, educator, visual storyteller, and Assistant Professor at the School of Planning and Architecture in New Delhi. He has taught at the Bartlett School of Architecture, University College London, where he conducted his PhD in Architectural History and Theory. Saptarshi's research lies at the intersections of architectural modernity, colonialism, and post-colonial studies. It focuses on connected histories and the movement of ideas, labor, and finance underlying architectural processes, thereby uncovering histories of architecture as a process and a collaborative act. His PhD thesis interrogates the categorization and classifications of architectural objects, investigating critiques of imperialism and international modernism in twentieth-century colonial India. He has lectured in and conducted workshops in more than twenty-five institutes all over India. His photographic work explores the poetics and mythologies embedded in everyday histories of human experience. He has published widely on modern heritage, knowledge systems and architectural history and theory, most recently writing for journals such as the *Architecture Research Quarterly* and *Architecture Beyond Europe*.

Cultural Studies

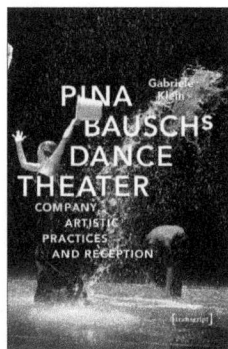

Gabriele Klein
Pina Bausch's Dance Theater
Company, Artistic Practices and Reception

2020, 440 p., pb., col. ill.
29,99 € (DE), 978-3-8376-5055-6
E-Book:
PDF: 29,99 € (DE), ISBN 978-3-8394-5055-0

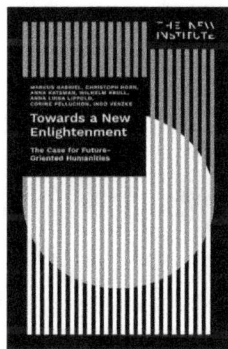

Markus Gabriel, Christoph Horn, Anna Katsman, Wilhelm Krull,
Anna Luisa Lippold, Corine Pelluchon, Ingo Venzke
**Towards a New Enlightenment –
The Case for Future-Oriented Humanities**

October 2022, 80 p., pb.
18,00 € (DE), 978-3-8376-6570-3
E-Book: available as free open access publication
PDF: ISBN 978-3-8394-6570-7
ISBN 978-3-7328-6570-3

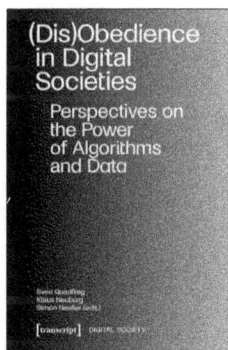

Sven Quadflieg, Klaus Neuburg, Simon Nestler (eds.)
(Dis)Obedience in Digital Societies
Perspectives on the Power of Algorithms and Data

March 2022, 380 p., pb., ill.
29,00 € (DE), 978-3-8376-5763-0
E-Book: available as free open access publication
PDF: ISBN 978-3-8394-5763-4
ISBN 978-3-7328-5763-0

**All print, e-book and open access versions of the titles in our list
are available in our online shop www.transcript-publishing.com**

Cultural Studies

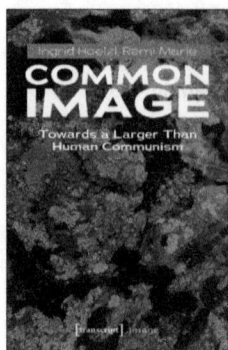

Ingrid Hoelzl, Rémi Marie
Common Image
Towards a Larger Than Human Communism

2021, 156 p., pb., ill.
29,50 € (DE), 978-3-8376-5939-9
E-Book:
PDF: 26,99 € (DE), ISBN 978-3-8394-5939-3

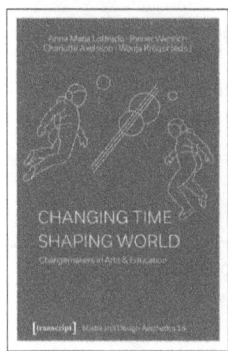

Anna Maria Loffredo, Rainer Wenrich,
Charlotte Axelsson, Wanja Kröger (eds.)
Changing Time – Shaping World
Changemakers in Arts & Education

September 2022, 310 p., pb., col. ill.
45,00 € (DE), 978-3-8376-6135-4
E-Book: available as free open access publication
PDF: ISBN 978-3-8394-6135-8

Olga Moskatova, Anna Polze, Ramón Reichert (eds.)
Digital Culture & Society (DCS)
Vol. 7, Issue 2/2021 –
Networked Images in Surveillance Capitalism

August 2022, 336 p., pb., col. ill.
29,99 € (DE), 978-3-8376-5388-5
E-Book:
PDF: 27,99 € (DE), ISBN 978-3-8394-5388-9

GPSR Authorized Representative: Easy Access System Europe, Mustamäe tee
50, 10621 Tallinn, Estonia, gpsr.requests@easproject.com